FEMINISTA
FREQUENCIES

COMMUNITY BUILDING THROUGH
RADIO IN THE YAKIMA VALLEY

MONICA DE LA TORRE

UNIVERSITY OF WASHINGTON PRESS

Seattle

Feminista Frequencies was made possible in part
by the University of Washington Press Authors Fund.

Design by Katrina Noble
Composed in Minion Pro, typeface designed by Robert Slimbach

Unless otherwise noted, all images courtesy of Rosa Ramón.

26   25   24   23   22   5   4   3   2   1

Printed and bound in the United States of America

UNIVERSITY OF WASHINGTON PRESS
uwapress.uw.edu

LIBRARY OF CONGRESS CATALOGING-IN-PUBLICATION DATA
Names: De La Torre, Monica, author.
Title: Feminista frequencies : community building through radio in the Yakima Valley /
Monica De La Torre.
Description: Seattle : University of Washington Press, [2022] | Series: Decolonizing feminisms
| Includes bibliographical references and index.
Identifiers: LCCN 2021015705 (print) | LCCN 2021015706 (ebook) | ISBN 9780295749679
(hardcover) | ISBN 9780295749662 (paperback) | ISBN 9780295749686 (ebook)
Subjects: LCSH: Community radio—Washington (State)—Yakima River Valley—History—
20th century. | Community development—Washington (State)—Yakima River Valley. |
Feminism—Washington (State)—Yakima River Valley. | Mexican Americans
Classification: LCC HE8698 .T67 2021 (print) | LCC HE8698 (ebook) |
DDC 384.5409797/57—dc23
LC record available at https://lccn.loc.gov/2021015705
LC ebook record available at https://lccn.loc.gov/2021015706

The paper used in this publication is acid free and meets the minimum requirements of
American National Standard for Information Sciences—Permanence of Paper for Printed
Library Materials, ANSI Z39.48–1984.∞

DECOLONIZING FEMINISMS
Piya Chatterjee, *Series Editor*

CONTENTS

Dedico este libro con mucho amor a Jovita Venegas de la Torre y Juan de la Torre.

Gracias por ser los mejores padres que siempre apoyaron mis sueños de ser escritora y la doctora.

ACKNOWLEDGMENTS

THE JOURNEY OF RESEARCHING, WRITING, AND LABORING A BOOK into existence is one that as a daughter of immigrants I never imagined could be a possibility, but it is a reality because of the village that nurtured my goals and replenished my spirit. I am eternally grateful to the following people, family, friends, collaborators, networks, and organizations who contributed to this project. Although this work bears my name as the sole author, the shared and created communal knowledge happened through the exchange of memories, stories, and past *conocimientos*. Yet any errors or oversights are entirely my own.

Thank you to everyone at Radio Cadena for their assistance. My heartfelt thank you to my collaborator and Chicana radio fairy godmother Rosa Ramón and Chuck Reinsch, as well as Amelia Ramón and Cecilia Ramón for their assistance and hospitality on our research trips to Granger, Washington. Thank you to Ricardo García and his family. I was introduced to the brilliant work of Radio Cadena by my doctoral advisor, Michelle Habell-Pallán, who valued my creative background in community radio and encouraged me to look into the herstories of Chicanas in broadcasting. Thank you to my dissertation committee, who helped me develop this work: Michelle Habell-Pallán, Shirley J. Yee, Susan J. Harewood, and Sonnet Retman.

At the University of Washington, the following provided funding, mentoring, and networking opportunities: GO-MAP, the University of Washington Center for the Study of the Pacific Northwest, Simpson Center for the Humanities (especially the Certificate in Public Scholarship), Miriam Bartha, John Vallier, and Rachel Arteaga. Thank you to the Women Who Rock Collective: through our work, I learned the meaning of a collective and communal scholar activist and *archivista* praxis. Thank you to Michelle Habell-Pallán and Sonnet Retman's collective feminist mentoring project, the Women Who Rock Graduate Mentoring Group, especially Deb Wong, Marisol Berríos-Miranda, Tiffany Ana López, Ann Powers, and

Maylei Blackwell. Thank you to the faculty and staff in the University of Washington's Department of Gender, Women and Sexuality Studies, especially Shirley J. Yee, Angela Ginorio, Sasha Su-Ling Welland, Amanda Lock Swarr, Priti Ramamurthy, Young Kim, and Catherine Richardson. To my intellectual *comadres, gracias por todo*: Martha Gonzalez, Noralis Rodríguez-Coss, Manoucheka Celeste, Sara Díaz, Jennifer McClearen, Miriam Valdovinos-Smith, and Melanie Hernandez.

My Chicana studies journey began at the University of California, Davis, in the Department of Chicana and Chicano Studies alongside scholars and students who continue to impact my work, especially Sergio de la Mora, who encouraged my passion for and love of film and culture. Thank you to all my mentors and femtors past and present who served as indispensable guides in my path: Lisceth Brazil-Cruz, Yvette Flores, Juana Mora, Cristina Ayala-Alcantar, Dolores Inés Casillas, Angela Ginorio, Ralina Joseph, and Ileana Rodríguez. Thank you to Jenny Stoever and the editors at *Sounding Out! The Sound Studies Blog*, for believing in my project early on and for first publishing my early work on Chicana radio activism. Thank you to the National Public Radio RAD Team, especially Laura Soto and Julie Rodgers.

Gracias to all of my *colegas* at Arizona State University, in the School of Transborder Studies, especially Edward Vargas, Brendan O'Conner, Eileen Díaz-McConnell, Patricia Corona, Victoria Villalba, and Marivel Danielson. Thank you also for support at ASU from the Institute for Humanities Research and the Faculty Fellows Program. *Gracias* to my intellectual *hermanas* of ASU's Faculty Women of Color Caucus, especially Ersula Ore, Vanessa Fonseca-Chávez, Mako Fitts-Ward, Chandra Crudup, and Carrie Sampson.

Thank you to my Soul Rebel Radio crew who helped me crack open a creative energy I did not know existed in me—you all rock: Lulu Kornspan, Miguel Paredes, Jorge Merino, Eduardo Arenas, Cristina Lopez, Carlos Rubio, Laura Cambron, Erick Iñiguez, and all past, present, and future Soul Rebels. To Anna and Montana Godinez, Olivia Paniagua, the best boss Christy Martinez, and the rest of the MALDEF *menudo familia*: thank you for your support. The process of starting and finishing this book benefited immensely from writing groups, both in person and now virtual, which sustained me through the highs and lows of academia and writing. Here I've learned to write alongside folks who care deeply about our stories and knowledge, while always working from a space of love, care, and radical imaginings of new worlds where many worlds fit. Thank you to all of my writing partners: Vanessa Fonseca-Chávez, Yessica García-Hernandez, Cati de los Rios, Sora Kim, and Amy Arguello. To my Zacatecas soul sister Sandra Castro Solis, *gracias* for your friendship and sharing your Chicana astronaut alien energy with me.

Thank you to the incredible staff at the University of Washington Press, especially Larin McLaughlin, Caitlin Alcorn, and Jason Alley. To the readers who posed questions and illuminated new paths for this work, thank you so much for your time and labor, including working through a pandemic to move this project along. I know I am missing many others: to everyone I missed listing here, thank you!

Thank you to all of my family and friends, including the De La Torre and Venegas families representing Jerez, Zacatecas, especially Araceli Caldera and Roxanna García. Thank you to my best friends and the cook-off crew: Connie and Lisa. Thank you to my Iowa family: Pam and Dan Woods, Gayle, Stephen, Calliope, and Barrett. Thank you to Paula Mendoza, the other future *doctora*. Thank you to my amazing siblings, the best brother and sister, who enrich my life with love, support, and adventure: Ana De La Torre and Jonathan De La Torre, *los quiero mucho. Mami y pa*, my parents, believed in and encouraged *mis sueños de ser doctora y profesora* from day one: thank you to my parents, Juan and Jovita. *Tengo la dicha de tener padres que por su esfuerzo, trabajo, y apoyo, juntos logramos una meta increíble.* To my partner, Scott Borton, for the encouragement, love, and unwavering belief that I could write a book, even when I didn't believe it: I love you.

ABBREVIATIONS

CPB   Corporation for Public Broadcasting

FCC   Federal Communications Commission

KDNA   Spanish-language radio station in Granger, Washington, on 91.9 FM; also referred to as Radio Cadena

NCEC   Northwest Communities Education Center

NCRN   Northwest Chicano Radio Network

NPR   National Public Radio

NRO   Northwest Rural Opportunities

CHRONOLOGY

1940s–1960s   Migrant farmworkers begin settling in Washington's Yakima Valley in greater numbers.

1968   Approximate date of the founding of Northwest Rural Opportunities (NRO).

1971   The Washington State Legislature approves the creation of the Commission on Mexican American Affairs.

Ricardo García is appointed the first executive director of the Commission on Mexican American Affairs.

1972   Ricardo García becomes the executive director of NRO.

1973   KBBF FM, Santa Rosa, California, the United States' first bilingual community radio station, goes on air.

1975   Julio César Guerrero and Dan Roble arrive in Washington State from Michigan and approach community organizations and activists to start a radio station or train farmworker youth to produce radio in Lynden, Washington, in collaboration with NRO. The project is called Radio Cadena.

1976   April—Founding of the Northwest Chicano Radio Network (NCRN) in Washington, Oregon, and Idaho. Articles of incorporation approved and signed on April 27, making NCRN and Radio Cadena a federally recognized 501(c)(3) nonprofit entity.

July—Radio Cadena airs on KRAB FM in Seattle, Washington. The radio station was housed from 1972 to 1980 in an abandoned fire station on First Hill in Seattle at 1406 Harvard Avenue.

1979   Radio Cadena makes its first radio broadcast as KDNA at 91.9 on the FM dial on December 19.

1980   Mount St. Helens erupts on May 18—KDNA goes on air warning farmworkers in the fields.

1980s   KDNA innovates community radio programming, especially with *radionovelas* like *La Esperanza del Valle* (*The Hope of the Valley*).

1986   Immigration Reform and Control Act (IRCA) enacted by the federal government.

1989   *Tres Hombres Sin Fronteras* produced by KDNA in collaboration with Novela Health Network; a groundbreaking *radionovela* about HIV/AIDS, it runs for fifteen episodes.

1990   Radio Cadena wins the Corporation for Public Broadcasting (CPB) Silver Award for *Tres Hombres Sin Fronteras*.

TERMINOLOGY

Chicana/o: I use "Chicana/o" for gender inclusivity. The terms "migrant" and "immigrant" are both deployed to add necessary nuance to communities of Mexican descent. The term "migrant" denotes persons traveling within the United States in search of labor, in this case farmwork. Within this study, many migrants of Mexican descent were US citizens and should not be conflated with the term "immigrant," which is reserved for persons emigrating to the United States. My use of terms such as "Mexican American," "Tejana/o," "Chicana," "Chicano," "Chicana/o," and "Latina/o" change throughout the book to reflect the historical time period being discussed. The book itself shows a trajectory of shifting meanings of language, the evolution of language and ideology, and the politics of linguistic representation, as well as the limitations of harnessing ethnic and racial categories for equity. For example, in chapters 1 and 2, I use "Chicano" and "Chicana," not "Chicanx," mindfully employing terms as they are recorded in the archive and were used in a particular historical moment. In the 1970s and 1980s, the term "Chicano public radio" appears in station documents and publications to describe the work of both women and men at emergent public radio stations.

feminista frequencies: I was introduced to the concept of feminist frequency through the work of feminist cultural critic Anita Sarkeesian (www.feminist frequency.com). While researching this book, I found that the tactics developed by Chicana radio broadcasters in the 1970s resonated with how Sarkeesian leveraged feminist critiques of patriarchal media gaming structures through the web series "Tropes vs. Women in Video Games," which reveals the persistence of misogyny in video games. For more on Anita Sarkeesian, feminist frequency, and other online feminist spaces see Janice Loreck's "Pleasurable Critiques: Feminist Viewership and Criticism in Feminist Frequency, Jezebel, and Rosie Recaps." My theorization of feminista frequencies is also inspired by radio scholar Kate Lacey's book *Feminine Frequencies: Gender, German Radio, and the Public Sphere, 1923–1945.*

FEMINISTA FREQUENCIES

LISTENING TO FEMINISTA FREQUENCIES

AS SOON AS AUTHORITIES ANNOUNCED THE IMPENDING THREAT of volcanic ash from the eruption of Mount St. Helens on the morning of May 18, 1980, KDNA FM began broadcasting news of the fiery eruption that killed fifty-seven people and destroyed 250 homes. A mere five months before the eruption, on December 19, 1979, KDNA's community radio broadcasters had transformed the 91.9 FM dial into one of the first full-time Spanish-language community radio stations in the United States, shifting the airwaves of the Yakima Valley's agricultural hub into a space where approximately 35,000 Spanish-speaking residents, especially farmworkers, could tune in for the latest emergency responses, news, music, and community-based programming.[1] KDNA's announcement about the eruption allowed farmworkers who were out in the fields at 8:39 a.m., when the explosion occurred, to seek safety from the harmful effects of the ash. Located in Granger, Washington, approximately eighty-five miles east of Mount St. Helens, KDNA was the only full-time Spanish-language media outlet in the region capable of reporting this catastrophic emergency to the region's Spanish-speaking farmworker community, which by the early 1980s consisted of both men and women in the fields. Station manager Rosa Ramón and staff acted quickly to start emergency broadcast services transmitting the news that "*¡Santa Helena ha eruptado! ¡Vayan a sus casas y sigan escuchando Radio KDNA!* (St. Helens has erupted! Go to your homes and stay tuned to KDNA for more information)."[2]

While the transmission on December 19 was technically KDNA's first broadcast on its newly licensed designation on the radio dial at 91.9 FM, just a few years earlier a group of Chicana and Chicano community activists, along with two radio producers hailing from Michigan, had begun radio production workshops with farmworker youth. This project created early iterations of Spanish programs that would later become KDNA's signature broadcasting mix of news, music, and cultural affairs. Radio Cadena—the name given to the project before the designated call letters of KDNA were established in 1979—first started in Lynden, Washington, in 1975 where radio producers Julio César Guerrero and Daniel Robleski (often shortened to Dan Roble) educated farmworker youth in radio production skills—a program sponsored by local community organization Northwest Rural Opportunities (NRO) headed by Ricardo García. Along with the other cofounders, KDNA's future station manager, Rosa Ramón—who also worked for NRO—recognized early on that access to radio broadcasting would have a significant impact on Mexican migrants and their families, especially women and farmworker youth, navigating new geographies and sociopolitical structures in the area. Soon the training program in Lynden would migrate to Seattle before settling in Granger, where KDNA established its own radio station studio in NRO's well-known three-story brick building with a former life of its own. Prior to the brick-and-mortar station being established in Granger, Radio Cadena was based in Seattle and transmitted Spanish-language programming with the help of community radio station KRAB FM (the details of which are found in chapter 1). Indeed, Radio Cadena's founders and volunteers tapped into institutional resources and already existing activist networks throughout the Pacific Northwest to successfully launch KDNA 91.9 FM.

The Mount St. Helens incident is just one early example of how Radio Cadena, including its staff and volunteers, served Mexican American and Chicano communities establishing roots in the Pacific Northwest. From educating farmworkers about the harmful effects of pesticides to empowering women to leave situations of domestic violence, KDNA quickly became a tool for community building, advocacy, and entertainment that was especially leveraged by the women who led it. For many of KDNA's women farmworkers-turned-broadcasters, developing skills in community radio production led to an awakening of personal agency and the brokering of new social relations both inside and outside the recording studio. The station's culturally relevant broadcasting, job training in radio production, and maintenance of Mexican and Tejana/o cultural traditions vis-à-vis radio programming and community events all worked to uplift farmworkers and their families, particularly women. This book traces the development of Spanish-language radio in the Yakima Valley as a tool for community building facilitated by the rise of community-based public broadcasting across the country alongside Chicano movement activity in the region.

THE BIRTH OF KDNA

In addition to its distinctive geography and weather, the Pacific Northwest was culturally distant from Mexican enclaves in the Southwest, as historian Mario Jimenez Sifuentez illuminates in *Of Forests and Fields: Mexican Labor in the Pacific Northwest*: "Place matters. The great distance between Mexican communities in the Northwest and other Mexican communities in the Southwest and Mexico provided challenges and opportunities for ethnic Mexicans."[3] Mexican communities in the Pacific Northwest lived in urban and rural areas without the traditional *barrios* or neighborhoods that publicly showcased Mexican pride and cultural identity via murals, grocery stores, bakeries, and community centers. The Pacific Northwest was unlike any other region that migrant farmworkers often encountered in their journeys through Texas, Arizona, and California. In the 1950s through the 1970s, migrant families had to work as units to make ends meet and often lived in substandard housing in migrant camps, making them vulnerable to communicable diseases. Farmworkers and their families were acutely vulnerable to working and living under conditions that perpetuated cycles of poverty and discrimination. These circumstances were often reinforced through the agribusiness structures of exploitation that, for example, paid workers by bushel or barrel or amount harvested instead of an hourly wage and housed them in "little shanty labor camps."[4]

In Washington State, before 1980, Seattle's Spanish-language programming was contained to a weekly two-hour block of music on Seattle public radio station KUOW: *Fiesta Musical*, hosted by Jose González on Saturdays. According to some Chicano movement activists, González's show focused exclusively on music, with resistance toward airing any content associated with Chicano movement activism, which included the work being done to secure a building to support the work of Chicano activists, community programming, social services, health care, and job placement through El Centro de la Raza in Beacon Hill.[5] In a 1973 television documentary, *Los Chicanos de Seattle (The Chicanos of Seattle)*, viewers see González setting up records for *Fiesta Musical* and hear host Elda Mendoza, in a voiceover tracked over footage inside the KUOW radio booth, state that he "is vehemently opposed to the Chicano movement and will not broadcast any material pertaining to Beacon Hill or associated efforts. There is of course nothing on local television nor is there a Spanish-language newspaper in Seattle."[6] Shortly after this documentary's production, Radio Cadena answered the call to air content about the Chicano movement and farmworker activism with the transmission of Spanish-language programming through Seattle-based community radio station KRAB FM's subsidiary communications authorization (SCA) signal from studios located in an old fire station on Capitol Hill.[7]

The documentary called out the lack of access to media outlets or news stories that centered on the lived experiences of Chicanos in Seattle or Washington. The ideology driving Chicano media activism championed equal access to the airwaves that could offer a space for resistance, not just complicit or passive easy listening. Similarly, media outlets for and about Chicana/o communities in Eastern Washington were practically nonexistent, and media coverage typically favored agribusinesses and growers' associations in the region, while major newspapers in the valley that were supportive of agribusinesses included the *Yakima Herald* and the *Yakima Daily Republic*.[8] KDNA opened the doors to people with no previous access to mass media and developed a production process that included men and women at all levels.

Staged alongside the Chicano movement in the Pacific Northwest, KDNA emerged as the leading advocate for farmworkers' rights in the region, especially by encouraging "workers to demand minimum wage, toilets in the field and water to wash pesticides from their hands before lunch. KDNA demands better conditions for migrant workers while keeping their culture alive."[9] Radio Cadena set out to be a station that provided news, information, and entertainment to Spanish-speaking listeners, while calling on Mexican farmworkers to build community often through direct participation with the radio station. Perhaps it was KDNA's unique and targeted outreach to farmworkers, often employed under terrible conditions, that worried growers in the region. For example, orchard owners "bombarded the Federal Communications Commission with claims the station was sparking worker rebellion," as Ricardo García, cofounder and KDNA's second and longest-serving station manager, recalls. "They realized now that we're not really inciting or promoting restlessness amongst farmworkers. What we're all about is information and education."[10] The intentional public support for farmworker families elevated by KDNA's radio programming is how the Chicano movement in the Pacific Northwest was heard on the airwaves.

For Mexican communities throughout the Yakima Valley, community radio was the platform where listeners congregated on-air in a space that was intentionally created with them as the target audience. Many of Radio Cadena's founders and broadcasters came from farmworker backgrounds, often with direct experiences and memories of working in the fields as children and young adults. KDNA's programming was driven by an awareness that community radio became a life-sustaining tool for farmworker communities across the Yakima Valley who were often exposed to pesticides while working in the fields. While there were also efforts to launch Spanish-language public service television programming and Spanish-language newspapers in the Yakima Valley, Radio Cadena was unmatched in its reach and popularity with Spanish-speaking listeners.[11] With KDNA, farmworkers now had access to information on resources to help them navigate structures of inequality, along with joyful music and whimsical programming that invited the entire family to listen to *la voz del campesino* (the voice of the farmworker).

Mexican farmworkers in the Yakima Valley who tuned their radios to 91.9 FM woke up to the sounds of *musica mexicana—rancheras, boleros,* and Tejano music—their transistor radio speakers blaring accordions, brass horns, and strings, perhaps transporting them back to the *Tejano conjunto bailes* (dances) they attended in the Rio Grande Valley in Texas.[12] Radio programming importantly provided news in Spanish about the Chicano community across the country through the Radio Cadena News Network, along with the latest weather and job openings for off-season employment. The impact these programs had on Spanish-speaking listeners across the Yakima Valley is that for the first time, educational, cultural, and informational programming spoke directly to their lived realities. Family programming, especially shows that could be enjoyed together, included *El Jardin de los Niños (Kindergarten), Recetas de Cocina (Kitchen Recipes)*, and *Biblioteca del Aire (Library of the Airwaves)*, along with announcements for community events. Through the daily morning programs that intentionally included children with *El Jardin de los Niños*, KDNA elevated children's voices on air, in Spanish, and offered an encouraging space of learning, imagination, and play, skills critical to child development. Hosts, both men and women from the community that listeners grew to have an intimate relationship with, having a dialogue with the community over the airwaves meant that Mexican Americans were finally able to access social services, especially for migrant farmworkers. Sundays were devoted to cultural programming representative of "the spirit of the people," including morning mass and an interview oral history program appropriately named *Historia Oral*: "This is part of Radio Cadena's cultural block. During this series Don Brisio Balderas, native of Piedras Negras, narrates his personal experiences in the Mexican Revolution. Don Balderas also discusses his present life and his experiences residing in South Seattle, Washington. This program is in line with the tradition of oral storytelling central to Mexican cultural practices."[13]

Significantly, cultural programs like *Arte de la Raza (Art of the People)*, *Raices Musicales (Musical Roots)*, and *Arriba el Telon (Raise the Curtain)* signaled a commitment to addressing the representational gap for Chicana/o artists, musicians, poets, and other cultural producers, an imperative that underpins much of the culturally centered Chicano movement activity across the United States.[14] Indeed, the inclusion of arts programming is directly tied to the explosion of art in Chicana and Chicano communities. Theater, public art like murals, and recognition and celebration of Mexican holidays such as Día de los Muertos (Day of the Dead), el día de la Virgen de Guadalupe, and deiciséis de Septiembre (Mexican Independence Day) became sonic touchstones on the airwaves for Mexican and Chicana/o communities in the Yakima Valley. The on-air recognition cultivated a community both on and off the airwaves. Radio allowed Chicano artists, poets, musicians, and other cultural workers, like Lydia Mendoza and Flaco Jimenez, to be integral to KDNA's programming and were key to drawing community to events held at the radio station. Sundays at the radio station often meant *tardeadas*, gatherings with music, food, and activities that provided residents with family-friendly activities while encouraging health and wellness in the community.

LAS MUJERES (THE WOMEN) AMPLIFYING KDNA

The production practices and labor behind these programs have resulted from the development and engagement with what I call *Chicana radio praxis*. Chicana radio praxis captures the radio work of community radio broadcasters who instituted a women-centered production process. At Radio Cadena, Chicanas such as station manager Rosa Ramón, producer Estella Del Villar, and news director Bernice Zuniga, along with other staff and volunteers, seeded a Chicana radio praxis by embodying formal leadership roles and producing programs targeting women listeners that broadcasted news stories, music, and informative programming by, for, and about farmworkers and working-class women of Mexican descent.[15] Ramón, along with KDNA's cofounders, employees, and volunteers, worked to build a radio station that welcomed everyone into the recording studio.[16] Producers like Del Villar were recognized early on as integral to the production process, yet often confronted a sexist environment that questioned their presence at the radio station.[17] For Chicana radio praxis to develop, men at KDNA also needed to support and encourage women's participation in radio production. My oral history interviews with KDNA's founders illuminate the collaborations between women and men at the station. Ricardo García recalls, "Women have been neglected in the radio business because of a machismo attitude among the managers and radio announcers. But we've discovered that women have more energy on their programs and can connect with women listeners."[18] Del Villar started as a secretary and receptionist while the station got under way in Seattle and soon moved up the ranks, becoming an instrumental producer of *radionovelas*, serialized educational radio dramas with a health or social message. Indeed, Chicana radio producers at KDNA played a pivotal role in developing and producing radio shows such as *Noticiero Radio Cadena (Radio Cadena News)*, which broadcasted local, regional, national, and international news throughout the day; shows dedicated to various musical genres; and children's programming through *El Jardín de los Niños*.

Women were bringing the organizational skills they developed in their community work as well as the gendered expectations of being a "good Mexican woman," especially mothers, which often translates to a responsibility for family wellness. Radio programs like *Voces del Barrio* (*Voices from the Community*) elevated the voices of Chicana and Chicano community leaders, as well as those of social workers and other health professionals who provided information about social and medical services available to farmworker families. Radio Cadena recognized that pregnant women were particularly vulnerable to the harms of pesticide poisoning that could result in birth defects or other diseases, which influenced early program decisions to air this content in programs like *Mujer* (*Woman*) and throughout the radio programming schedule. Moreover, this inspired Chicana radio producers to include facts about health and wellness in public service announcements and *radionovelas,* with topics ranging from breast-feeding to asthma.

My use of "Chicana" in describing this radio praxis calls attention to the historical specificity and theoretical orientations of this project: the term signals an explicit Chicana feminist positioning and calls out a particular historical period of civil rights activism—the Chicano movement. To be clear, I am not claiming that this Chicana radio praxis is exclusive to women; rather, I use the term to deliberately center a practice that I argue emerged out of creating radio programming that centered Chicana lived realities. We know very little about Chicanas and Latinas in public broadcasting,

particularly community radio, so this book (and the accompanying podcast) begin the work of (re)recording their contributions and inserting them
as key actors into a rich history of building institutions of public broadcasting based in community and belonging since the early days of community
radio.[19] In recovering their story and that of others they inspired, *Feminista
Frequencies* tells the mostly silenced history of how Chicanas and Latinas
cultivated a community radio practice that fused creative cultural productions with news and practical everyday programming in Spanish that was
inclusive of a wide range of listeners including men, women, and children.
My focus on Chicanas in public broadcasting also introduces women's
activism through community radio into the growing body of scholarship
on Chicana and Mexicana organizing and political work.[20]

In 2012 I met and interviewed Radio Cadena cofounder and station
manager Rosa Ramón for the Women Who Rock Digital Oral History
Archive, and as a former community radio producer myself, I reveled in
learning about women like me, first-generation Chicana college students
and activists turned community media producers who launched an entire
radio station with the goal of reaching the Chicano community.[21] This first
interview evolved into a personal and professional relationship that significantly impacted my approach to researching and writing about community radio. Rosa and I have since collaborated to find and preserve
Radio Cadena's legacy as well as the work of the women who created what
we now recognize as Chicano community radio and what scholars and
activists call the Chicano Media Movement.[22] We traveled to Radio Cadena
in search of any traces of the station's institutional history, and Ramón
connected me to a community of former and current KDNA radio producers as well as other Chicano community radio broadcasters, including
women who led these stations in the early days of community radio. We
have presented at conferences and on virtual panels where Ramón has
shared the significance of my own involvement in community radio to our
archival work.[23]

In order to build a Chicana/o Community Radio Archive, I have worked
closely with Ramón after our 2012 interview, collaborating in search of key
station documents, and she has generously shared her own personal archive.
Our archival processes draw from feminist methodological practices that
stress reflexivity, reciprocity, and community building as integral to the
archival process referred to as "archivista praxis" by the Women Who Rock
(WWR) Collective. The term "archivista" is a fusion of "archivist and activist practices to rethink the collective possibilities of the archive, deliberately

employing the networked archive as a tool to document and create the conditions of possibility for social change. Here we [WWR] use the term 'networked' to highlight the human relationships that connect people and communities working on related projects with similar aims."[24] I learned archivista skills, especially expanding the archive to include the work of women in creative production like media, as a member of the WWR Collective. As a Chicana radio activist, Ramón models feminist collaboration and understands the importance of documenting one's history. The extensive photographic archive is also due in large part to Ramón's personal interest in photography and her purchase of a camera that documented KDNA's early days.

This book, then, does not just elaborate on a history; it mobilizes Chicana radio praxis as a methodology by building relationships with former Chicana and Chicano radio producers, identifying sound in nonauditory artifacts, and creating new archives. In practicing this methodology, Rosa Ramón and I have uncovered a rich archive of audio and video recordings, radio-tower blueprints, newspaper articles, photographs, board-meeting minutes, and program guides that together demonstrate the process of creating radio programs and how it happens at the level of production. Indeed, the materials in our expanding self-created archive propelled my analysis of what happens behind the scenes and the microphone, a process of making community radio that reveals the nuances of how broadcasters brought innovative content to the airwaves.[25] This book underscores how the archival record created by Chicana administrative staff, record keepers, and secretaries is significant in the preservation of institutional histories and centers their work as key to the archival process.[26] Chicana radio praxis insists on "keeping records" just as it relies on broadcasting or playing records, including music and programming not heard on other airwaves. For example, while working as KDNA's station manager, Rosa conserved important documents and took many photographs with a newly purchased camera, creating an archive in the moment, which I can now mine for a history of Chicano community radio. The archive is also an instrument that gets played and silenced in various ways.

FEMINISTA FREQUENCIES

The Chicana radio praxis fostered at KDNA then led to the emission of *feminista frequencies*, feminist radio waves that we can still hear and tap into to this day if we know how and what to listen for. As a concept, feminista frequencies is both an epistemological tool and an intervention that tunes readers and listeners into the participation of Chicanas and Latinas in creating and running community radio stations that remain on air to this day. In doing this work of recapitulating KDNA's history alongside Rosa, I recognized myself and my own work in collective media production as part of the larger legacy and impact of feminista frequencies, even though I had not heard of KDNA or their work until beginning this project. And now I see and hear feminista frequencies in the explosion of Latinx podcasts—podcasts produced by Chicana and Latinas who are adapting Chicana radio praxis to digital online environments. Moreover, the products (radio programs, program guides, and photographs) created by Chicana and Chicano radio producers are also conceived as feminista frequencies. The approach to community radio production, the process of getting programs on air, the way radio was produced is what I call Chicana radio praxis, resulting in feminista frequencies. Feminista frequencies are disruptions; feminista frequencies "disrupt traditional epistemological boundaries and informs how we develop and enact the research process."[27]

In this book I refer to "frequencies" in terms of their actual function in radio broadcasting as electromagnetic waves of sound, as well as a metaphor for social movement activism. Here, radio frequencies carry discourses of resistance and track migrant movement across the United States (Texas Mexican migration between the Southwest and the Pacific Northwest) and across borders (Mexican immigration to the United States). Radio frequencies expand our understanding of Chicana/o community formations in the United States.[28] I also understand frequencies as the way community radio transmitted production tactics or the ways we enact collective media-making across temporalities and geographies. For communities of Mexican descent, radio frequencies become another instrument that can be played in many ways: radio is an instrument of communication and community building that is vital to activists' projects.

A study of radio, and in particular community radio, requires a nuanced articulation of the various components of radio: Radio is a technology. Radio is sound. Radio is the organizations or groups behind its production. Radio is also about listeners—and, in this study, communities of reception. Radio is also about the industry structures and policies regulating its production. Radio is also a strategic choice in communication technology that brings various constituencies together on one platform.

Frequencies connect the shared radio work by Chicano public radio stations. Frequencies are about transformations—the physical transformation of radio waves to the sound emanating from radio speakers or headphones as well as the personal and community transformations that directly result from access to mass communication like radio. Regionally, creating a channel to the FM radio frequencies undoubtedly transformed radio heard in the area, while also impacting the lives of those who produced and listened to the programming that reached Spanish-speaking farmworkers and the emergent Mexican American and Chicano community in the Yakima Valley. Frequencies, therefore, are apt in describing the community transformations that occurred as a result of KDNA's radio broadcasts. For marginalized communities, radio is a more accessible medium than visual (television and film) and print (newspapers, magazines, and books) media because of its low cost and accessibility.[29] The skills needed to produce radio are more easily replicable, especially compared to television and film, which have more significant technical barriers for entry, particularly for minoritized groups.

This story and the Chicana radio praxis developed at KDNA are not unique to this station but form part of a larger network of Chicano and Chicana public community radio broadcasting launched in the late 1960s and 1970s. Additionally, in the process of researching and writing this book, I realized that Chicana radio praxis was found in my own work in the 2000s when I joined radio collective Soul Rebel Radio working out of KPFK 90.7 FM in Los Angeles. Indeed, while this book grounds its analysis in Radio Cadena, Chicana radio praxis is found at other stations and in the lasting impact of the feminista frequencies it produced. Chicana and Chicano community radio producers often came from the same communities they intended to reach through their broadcasts and were already involved in some form of community activism.[30] Activists created and produced women-centered community radio programs like *Mujer* at KDNA and *Somos Chicanas* (*We Are Chicanas*) at bilingual station KBBF FM in Santa Rosa, California.

I deliberately deploy the term "*feminista*" in Spanish not only to denote the bilingualism heard throughout Chicana/o radio programming as well as in current iterations of feminista frequencies in sonic storytelling like podcasts, but also to signal the Chicana feminist foundations of this project. During the 1960s and 1970s, US women of color activists, scholars, and cultural workers were talking back to power and hegemony across platforms by harnessing a common language and identifying "common grounds on which to make coalitions across their own profound cultural, racial, class, sex, gender, and power differences."[31] The theoretical insights and alternative epistemological practices enacted in and through Chicana feminisms—borderlands theories, embodied knowledge, and creative expression—provide a vast archive of theoretical, epistemological, and methodological tools to excavate alternative sites of knowledge production. Chicana and Latina feminists bridge multiple identities and social practices because they "come from a long line of workers, activists, theorists, and writers within their respective Latino communities."[32]

The feminized popular saying *calladita te ves mas bonita* (you look prettier when you're quiet) is a patriarchal tool used against women to elicit our silence and prevent us from vocalizing our agency. Chicana community radio broadcasters challenged established racial, gendered, and class hierarchies in media production and representation by centering the voices and experiences of farmworker women of Mexican descent. They vowed to change radio by reimagining who was behind the microphone and on the other side of the radio speaker. The widespread call for participation from farmworkers—including women, children, and men with little to no radio broadcasting skills—to embody both listener and producer was sound-breaking. Indeed, as bell hooks profoundly states, "Moving from silence into speech is for the oppressed, the colonized, the exploited, and those who stand and struggle side by side a gesture of defiance that heals, that makes new life and new growth possible. It is that act of speech, of 'talking back,' that is no mere gesture of empty words, that is the expression of our movement from object to subject—the liberated voice."[33] Chicana radio broadcasters encountered patriarchal and male-centered production practices that policed their participation at the radio station, especially for women with more public roles like station managers, producers, and on-air personalities. These negotiations played out in the programming and in the development of collective media production practices where women insisted their voices be carried on the airwaves not just as unpaid volunteers but as *employed* producers of content.

MEXICAN AMERICAN RADIO: WHY RADIO MATTERS TO COMMUNITIES OF MEXICAN DESCENT

Unraveling Radio Cadena's founding and narrating its history as a station devoted to creating unique Spanish-language broadcasts for migrant farmworkers in the Yakima Valley requires situating readers within the importance of radio for Chicano communities and the unique world of community media. Mexicans and Mexican Americans have a deeply rooted relationship to radio that predates the onset of community-based public broadcasting of the 1960s and 1970s. Radio is a vital cultural practice central to understanding Mexican American and Chicana/o experiences in the United States. The history of Mexicans and Mexican Americans in radio broadcasting on both sides of the US-Mexico border dates back to radio's early days when, in the 1920s and 1930s, Mexican and Latino brokers purchased blocks of airtime for Spanish-language programming at predominantly commercial English-language radio stations.[34] The first successful brokers included Señor Lozano, who began a brokered program in San Antonio in 1928. In 1946 Raul Cortez, a Spanish-language radio broker, became the first Chicano to own and operate the first full-time Spanish-language radio station, KCOR, in San Antonio, Texas.[35] Similarly, broker Paco Sanchez moved on to own a full-time Spanish-language radio station in Denver, Colorado, while others like Rodolfo Hoyos, who was on air in Los Angeles from 1932 to 1974, would become employees of the stations that previously carried their voices on purchased airtime.[36]

The late 1930s witnessed an increase of Spanish-language programming on radio stations throughout the Southwest. In fact, the International Broadcasting Company, based in El Paso, Texas, began producing and selling Spanish programming to various stations in the United States.[37] One of the first Spanish-language radio personalities in Los Angeles was Pedro J. González, who migrated from Mexico to the United States in the 1920s.[38] González's technical skills as a telegraph operator for Mexican Revolution leader Pancho Villa perhaps served him well when he was hired by an English-language radio station in Los Angeles to read commercials in Spanish. In the 1930s, González became the host for the Spanish-language program *Los Madrugadores (The Early Risers)*. By 1941 Spanish-language programming, which included music, news, radio dramas, and talk shows, was being broadcast in places such as New York, Texas, Arizona, and California.[39] As scholar Deborah Vargas notes, these Spanish radio blocks played an important role in aurally imagining, creating, and capturing an audience through song, vocals, and sounds, but it also became an aural site of Mexicana (Mexican women) representations through the live performances of artists like Rosita Fernández.[40] As commercial radio developed, women not only performed over the airwaves, they filled critical gaps in programming as on-air hosts and producers.

For instance, the first woman disc jockey in Phoenix, Arizona was Graciela Gil Olivarez, who worked at Spanish-language radio station KIFN. In the Pacific Northwest, Herminia Méndez hosted the first Spanish-language program in Sunnyside, Washington, in 1951. Méndez traveled with her family as migrant farmworkers from Eagle Pass, Texas, and settled in the Pacific Northwest in 1948. Méndez soon recognized the need for Spanish radio programming and, with no prior radio experience, boldly approached KREW's station manager to air Mexican music.[41] While more research and information on these women is needed to fully comprehend the impact of their work, their contributions and innovations on commercial radio through Spanish-language programming is a precursor to the work picked up by Chicana radio broadcasters in Chicano community radio discussed in this book. Foundational scholarship in the area of commercial and community Spanish-language radio broadcasting is elevated in works by Dolores Inés Casillas and Mari Castañeda, who have shaped the field by tuning us to the importance of Latino radio listeners, Spanish-language radio's potent ability to advocate on behalf of Latina/o communities, and the significance of Spanish-language radio industry writ large.[42] This book continues this work by tracing the development of community radio broadcasting that expanded the radio dial, making room for Chicano and Chicana voices.

The development and proliferation of portable transistor radios changed when and where people accessed the airwaves, especially for workers who listened to the radio at work. As radio scholar Susan Douglas demonstrates, "as radio became more portable—and between 1949 and 1960 the number of portable sets made by U.S. companies quadrupled, while the number of imported Japanese transistor sets increased sevenfold—it accompanied people everywhere, to the beach, to work, in the backyard and on buses, cars, and subways."[43] For farmworkers, this meant that they could now bring radios with them into the fields while at work. "Many of the workers take small radios with them into the fields," said Tomas Cerna, a Toppenish, Washington, resident and member of the state's Commission on Mexican-American Affairs enacted in 1971. "It's the main thing that keeps them informed. Some of the workers come from Mexico and can't read."[44] KDNA and other rural Chicano community radio stations like KBBF FM in Santa Rosa, California, leveraged this medium to build stations committed to programming for these farmworkers.

Radio listening practices were strongly cemented among migrant farmworkers by the time Chicano community radio went on air in the 1970s.

Future founders and employees of Chicano community radio stations recalled childhood in Texas, in places along the border like the Rio Grande Valley, where radio transmitters could tap into Mexican radio stations like the famous XEW broadcasting from Mexico City.[45] Mexican radio stations are recognized for their powerful transmissions. Popular superpowered "border radio" stations had sprung up along the US-Mexico border in the 1930s.[46] Ricardo García, Radio Cadena cofounder, recalls his childhood in Texas and the strength of Mexican airwaves reaching his receiver in his hometown of San Diego, an early exposure to the creative power of radio that would later greatly influence his work at Radio Cadena. García recalls, "I remember those days in Texas listening to XEW, because Mexico has some excellent live radio shows. XEW was a powerful radio station, especially after seven o'clock at night. We used to listen to the live programs, and I think that created an awareness and skill-building in my mind."[47] This strong connection to radio broadcasting primed García, along with many Mexican Americans and Chicanos, to innovate in the noncommercial world of radio broadcasting when President Lyndon B. Johnson signed the 1967 Public Broadcasting Act. This legislation, coupled with Mexican Americans' enthusiasm and willingness to innovate on the radio airwaves, opened a new world of possibilities for Chicana and Chicano community broadcasters, a history expanded on in chapter 1.

CHICANO PUBLIC RADIO ACTIVATES THE AIRWAVES

While Chicano and Mexican immigrant communities in the United States have leveraged commercial radio airwaves to their advantage, the rise of community radio along with civil rights organizing in the 1960s and 1970s encouraged Chicana and Chicano activists to create their own radio stations. Noncommercial radio in the form of educational broadcasting has existed in some form since the introduction of radio technologies in the 1920s. However, community radio as it was imagined in the late 1960s–'70s within a zeitgeist of civil rights and social change offered a unique entry point for anyone to imagine themselves as radio producers. Within the conditions of possibility for community radio broadcasting in this historic moment, media activists argued that media industries were not representative of diverse audiences, particularly Black and Latino communities, who took legal action that included petitions to deny broadcast license renewals.[48] KDNA's ethos of community broadcasting is described by Rosa Ramón:

The staff and volunteers who were on the air came from the same communities that we wanted to serve. A warm relationship was created. It was like a family. And that's the way it should be. Community radio is about people. If there isn't an open door, then community radio isn't doing what it's supposed to be doing. Radio waves were supposed to belong to the people, and I think that's the whole philosophy of community radio. It's part of the community and they take care of, support, and trust what's theirs. The very special bond that can exist between community radio and its listeners, I believe, is very difficult to achieve with other mediums.[49]

As Ramón explains, alternative, noncommercial stations fostered an intimate connection engendered by a model of media production that cast producers as listeners and listeners as producers. As they were working to get KDNA on the air, KDNA's station manager and director of programming created promotional materials to get the word out about shows coming to their radio dials. A *Radio Cadena Fact Sheet* explains how this alternative to commercial radio worked, "Since the sponsors of community radio are the listeners, programming is determined by listeners' needs and not only by advertisers' dollars. Therefore, community radio is able to offer a wide variety of musical, cultural, informational and educational programs. Community radio also provides access to groups that traditionally do not have access to the media such as other minorities, farmworkers, women or any other nonprofit organizations. Talk shows, call-in shows, and local news programs will deal with issues of importance to these groups and allow for community input."[50] This allows radio stations to air diverse programming not typically heard on mainstream radio, such as interviews, political commentary, dramatic sketches, audio documentaries, poetry, satire, and listener call-ins.[51]

This free-form programming style allows for a more fluid dialogue between announcers and listeners. In many instances, the announcer has the opportunity to be the listener and vice versa. That is, community radio and the people involved in creating these radio programs are representative of a particular community—in the case of Radio Cadena, it was Chicana and Chicano migrant farmworkers. Community radio station announcers and hosts were typically not professionals; they were members of communities that were either not represented or misrepresented in mainstream radio. Whereas mainstream media largely ignored or vilified Mexican American or Chicano political unrest and social activism, Chicano community radio broadcasts aired more nuanced, diverse perspectives on socioeconomic conditions and Chicano cultural lived experience. On KDNA and across the Chicano-owned and -operated stations, listeners engaged in a lively exchange of opinions and ideas related to, for example, the political activism related to farmworkers and other working-class Spanish-language-dominant communities. While Spanish-language radio brokers in the 1920s–'30s had purchased airtime on commercial radio in time slots ranging from thirty minutes to two hours,[52] the community radio format allowed for an entire programming day specifically dedicated Chicana/o broadcasting.

The Public Broadcasting Act marked a new phase in the national movement for media reform and provided an entry point for Chicano community radio stations to emerge in the 1970s and '80s, starting in 1973 with KBBF FM in Santa Rosa, California (the nation's first bilingual noncommercial radio station). In April 1976, a tristate radio network between Washington, Oregon, and Idaho was incorporated as a 501(c)(3) nonprofit entity under the name of the Northwest Chicano Radio Network (NCRN) with the official title of Radio Cadena.[53] While it never fully materialized into the tristate community radio network the founders originally intended, Radio Cadena continued producing programs in Seattle and launched a national Spanish-language news network that produced and circulated original segments for commercial and noncommercial radio stations across the United States. KDNA, which grew out of Radio Cadena, was founded in 1979, and Radio Bilingüe (KSJV FM in Fresno, California) started in 1980, among other noncommercial radio stations.[54]

The stories covered by Chicano community radio stations shifted the narrative about Mexican American communities in the United States. Community radio programming expanded the national conversation that too often silenced Chicana/o voices. The movement to create radically different nonstereotypical representations of Chicanas and Chicanos across media platforms, dubbed the Chicano Media Movement, has been documented and analyzed by Francisco J. Lewels, Chon Noriega, and Dolores Inés Casillas.[55] In particular, the 1974 publication of *The Uses of the Media by the Chicano Movement* by scholar and media activist Lewels clearly links the vital role of media within Chicana- and Chicano-led social movements. "Armed with the knowledge provided them by the public-interest law groups," Lewels elaborates, "Chicanos began looking toward the electronic media in the late 1960s as a primary objective in their civil rights movement."[56] Scholar Randy J. Ontiveros explains this phenomenon: "Mindful of the culture industry's growing power, activists responded with the creation of an independent Chicano/a media that used mimeograph machines, offset printing, and other available media technologies to circulate alternative images and narratives of Mexican America. The Chicano/a media took many different expressions, including film, television, radio, and other forms of communication."[57]

In exploring how Chicana/o radio activists and cultural workers in the Pacific Northwest were able to voice their belonging and presence in US culture through community radio programs, I heed Casillas's call to build on these important works. As she notes, "The development of bilingual community radio in rural areas should encourage scholars to recast the era's Chicano media movement beyond urban centers to include the media activity of bilingual radio in rural settings."[58] By 1985, three of the five Chicano-owned and -operated community radio stations in the United States were led by *mujeres*, women station managers responsible for daily operations, including technical, business, and administrative management. Station managers Margarita García from KUBO in Salinas, California; Eva Torres from KMPO in Modesto, California; and Rosa Ramón from KDNA in Granger, Washington, were all leaders in the emergent Chicano public radio industry. Chicanas played an indispensable role in founding community radio stations with an ethos of inclusion and community participation.

"Chicano public radio," a term utilized by station managers that, as Casillas argues, "characterize[d] their early station identity, indicative of the political moment's focus on taking back the public airways as well as invoking the Mexican American population as Chicanos,"[59] cracked open the "public" in public broadcasting to include Spanish-dominant listeners, breaking the monolingual trend in radio centering on English, to run an entire day of programming in Spanish. In the efforts of emerging Chicana and Chicano radio producers to participate in the creation of community-based radio broadcasting, the pressing question was not *if* they could make radio but, rather, *how* they would utilize community radio broadcasting to serve their communities. The establishment of community-based radio stations like KDNA was fueled by national media reform trends as well as regional and national collaborations among nonprofit civil rights groups. KBBF, which was founded by Sonoma State University undergraduates and farmworkers, shared KDNA's goal of bringing communications technologies to farmworkers in the region, an aim that facilitated a connection among the stations. Indeed, when the KDNA founders were in the process of starting their station, they turned to KBBF's founders and volunteers for advice.[60] Chicano community radio stations wanted each other to thrive, and they shared resources that helped many of these stations get off the ground and fill the gap of programming for Spanish-speaking and bilingual audiences.

Community-based programming at Chicano stations worked to include holistic and comprehensive radio shows addressing the health, employment, and cultural needs of Mexican American communities. KBBF's bilingual and bicultural programming included shows like *Hora Médica (Health Hour), Chicano Youth and the Law,* NPR news in English, and *Women's Spaces.* KDNA's programming consisted of shows like *El Jardin de los Niños, Raíces Culturales (Cultural Roots),* and *Oportunidades de Trabajo (Job Opportunities).* The community radio activists and broadcasters like those at KDNA and KBBF FM were committed to transforming the airwaves to sound out locally produced programming that addressed the needs of Chicana/o and farmworkers in isolated rural communities like Santa Rosa, California, and Granger, Washington. This resulted in KDNA being referred to as *la voz del campesino* and KBBF FM as *la voz del pueblo* (the voice of the people). These monikers were constitutive of the emergent Chicano public radio. Radio Cadena took on a more activist approach when planning early programming, with shows dedicated to bridging the community to social services and government social programs: "Radio Cadena hopes with the interests and support of its listeners and local community agencies to act as a catalyst for the uplift of the spirit of the Chicano, Latino, and Hispanic of the eighties"[61]—a message emphasized throughout the programs produced by KDNA.

As community radio stations began to infiltrate the airwaves with radically different content, bilingual Mexican American youth could tune their radio dials to the brand-new sounds of Chicano public radio stations sprouting up in more rural places. Changing the dial and landing on something you've never heard before is an experience that public radio broadcaster María Martin fondly remembers. Before diving into the world of community radio as a producer and on-air talent at stations like KBBF FM, NPR, and KUOW in Seattle, Washington, Martin discovered Chicano radio's unique potential in the mid-1970s. "In the wine country of northern California, I was absentmindedly turning the radio dial when I heard something I'd never, *ever* heard before: it was in English *and* in Spanish." Martin recalls that "the station [KBBF FM] played reggae, *rancheras*, and *dedicas* [dedications] on the oldies show and covered public affairs. For the first time in my life, I heard media that reflected my reality as a bilingual and bicultural person of Mexican *and* American heritage. . . . I was hooked on this pioneering little radio station and on making radio that cut across cultural lines."[62] Martin was in awe when she heard, for the first time, radio programming that bridged her bicultural lived experiences.

Similarly, for community radio broadcaster Ernesto Aguilar, listening to public radio meant discovering new identities, different forms of identification, and group belonging:

> Through public media, I found myself coming back to listen to the news, to hear music I never knew existed—the blues, y'all, seriously—and to have my little teenage world expanded far beyond anything I had ever imagined. For me, that late-night stumbling onto an iconoclastic corner of radio changed my life and made me who I am. I'm the only person in my family to get a college degree, and public media motivated my studies in journalism. My passion for communities was stoked by the evocative radio voices that ushered me through my high school years. Without public media, my future would have most assuredly been an uncertain one.[63]

Aguilar conveys a sentiment that many community radio broadcasters expressed about public broadcasting that inspired many to enter the recording studio. This life-changing medium opens doors to educational opportunities and inspires career trajectories into fields like journalism and the public service sectors. It offers community involvement and educational services on wide-ranging topics, including immigration naturalization services and health. After the passage of the Immigration Reform and Control Act in 1986, Radio Cadena served as an information hub over the airwaves, while the radio station became a central application services zone for nearly 8,000 people. It was selected by the state's Department of Social and Health Services to carry out Washington's information and education campaign about IRCA. Northwest Communities Education Center combined radio information dissemination with its services that included assistance with filling out forms and submitting necessary documentation.

CHICANA RADIO PRAXIS AS METHOD

Despite tremendous interest in the areas of Latina/o media studies and feminist media studies, there is a distressingly small body of work dedicated exclusively to the study of Chicana/o or Spanish-language community radio in the United States. *Feminista Frequencies: Community Building through Radio in the Yakima Valley* adds a much-needed perspective on community radio and extends studies primarily centered on commercial US Spanish-language radio.[64] This book provides an in-depth mixed-methods analysis of how Chicana and Chicano organizers–turned–community radio broadcasters used public radio beginning in the 1970s to educate, entertain, and build community over the airwaves. It offers a rare glimpse into public broadcasting by centering the vantage point of Chicana community radio producers who made inroads into highly selective male-dominated public media structures as leaders of community radio stations, while building systems of support and spaces for women to master radio production. By engaging in a Chicana radio praxis methodology, one that centered the collective creation of an archive with Rosa Ramón and other Chicano community radio broadcasters, I also contribute to a larger epistemological project that addresses erasures of Chicanas and Chicanos in community radio broadcasting. The archiving process and narrative I track in this book—feminista frequencies—by amplifying women's work also appears in the archival work for this project. The task of archiving and preserving our stories is a feminist project. The archival process also served a twofold purpose: we scanned, collected, and digitized materials that were at risk of being lost or erased, and archiving tasks activated and deepened my relationship with community radio broadcasters. I arrived at the process of archiving from my experiences as a radio producer before graduate school.

Rosa Ramón is a scholar's dream collaborator. As a Chicana radio activist, she models feminist collaboration and understands the importance of documenting one's history. In her five years as station manager, Ramón kept meticulous records of KDNA's activity that now serve as archival records of the station's sonic activity. She used her own camera and film to document the process of getting the station off the ground—literally with images of building the tower—and of the people involved and the building that first housed KDNA. These images are powerful evidence of the early days of the station. This is of particular significance for a medium that is mostly aural and oral and with few audio archives; these images offer the opportunity to see what we cannot hear. Missing aural artifacts such as recorded programs offer exciting opportunities to enact feminist methodologies that remind us to look at what's not said, what is missing, and what is silenced in the third spaces of knowledge production. I turn to the visual—program guides, correspondence—to hear the sonic: program titles, music played, what's discussed on air. The title of a radio program—while devoid of any acoustic texture—provides evidence so that we can reimagine and reconstruct how KDNA sounded and continues to sound.

We interpret the historical record and simultaneously create new epistemologies when we enact feminist methodological tactics.

In this book, I interweave my knowledge as a former community radio producer with new archival data (including an online digital archive), oral history interviews, and textual analysis to reveal how community broadcasting for Spanish-dominant and bilingual Mexican American and Chicana/o audiences transformed the airwaves. Radio Cadena's legacy in crafting a public voice for newly politicized Chicanas and Chicanos has been silenced from the historical record or marginalized by hegemonic narratives of public broadcasting. As a Chicana feminist with a background in community-based collective radio production, my intimacies with this work reveal a scholar activist praxis that produces new evidence, archives, and insights into the radio-based soundwork carried out by Chicana and Chicano farmworkers, students, and community activists. Moreover, given my own added layer of analysis as a radio producer (elaborated on in chapter 3), I foreground these levels of embeddedness by demonstrating how community media production necessitates a network of producers, listeners, community, media, and government organizations and policies, and transnational mediated practices. That is, KDNA's emergence onto the scene of community radio pulls back the curtains on the work and the collaborations, including challenges and achievements, necessary to make radio.

This feminist methodology connects a shared frequency of community-based feminist media praxis historically found in radio to current forms of digital media and podcasting. While centered on radio, I also narrate much broader sociopolitical dynamics animated by civil rights–era Chicana/o and feminist political agendas and discourses. Placing Chicana and Chicano community radio activists into a more amplified cultural and historical context underscores a praxis of Chicana/o community media production rooted in migration, social movement activism, and the fight to have equal access to public radio broadcasting. I present a critical lost *herstory* of Chicanas and Latinas who were instrumental in the development of community radio, particularly approaching radio studies from a Chicana feminist framework. Due in large part to a lack of research on Spanish-language radio generally, and Chicano community radio more specifically, the growing narrative risks casting the Chicano Media Movement as male dominated when we only recognize, document, and historicize the work of influential male radio broadcasters and journalists.[65]

I focus on Mexican American communities in the Pacific Northwest, a region that gets very little interest as a critical site of Chicana/o community building, activism, and cultural production. By zeroing in on the Yakima Valley and Radio Cadena, I shed light on a vanguard of Chicana/o community media broadcasters who made radio a unique space that intentionally incorporates farmworker men and women, who previously did not have at their disposal a system of mass communication and connectivity. Indeed, I build on literature demonstrating how radio has historically served as a lifeline for marginalized communities, revealing how media, and Spanish-language radio in particular, continue to be embedded in our everyday lives.[66]

CHAPTER OVERVIEWS

The story of how Radio Cadena came into existence, coupled with a detailed analysis of the larger Chicana/o community radio broadcasting network, demonstrates how media activists joined forces with state and community-based organizations to create pathways that established the first Chicana/o-owned and -operated full-time Spanish-language community radio station in the United States. By tapping into already existing cultural and political infrastructures or frequencies, KDNA not only leveraged much-needed financial and organizational support from these groups but also created a foundational base of listeners and content producers comprised of people already involved in these networks. The early beginnings of Chicano community radio remind us that media and representation have always been contested spaces for Mexican American and Chicana communities, who continue to fight for richer and more complex narratives or for media that simply acknowledge us as a key demographic of listeners. However, as this book showcases, the early days of Chicano community radio sparked a cultural practice and network of Latina and Latino radio producers, including a women-centered Chicana radio praxis (detailed in chapter 2) and programming aesthetic rooted in *rasquache* (do-it-yourself) principles that I later learned as a community radio producer in the 2000s (discussed in chapter 3). Central is a focus on Chicana/o radio content and production—that is, how did Chicana and Chicano radio producers make the work happen and what drove and inspired the content production? These questions led me to further explore the frequencies produced out of the lived experiences of Chicana, Mexican American, and Tejana and Tejano farmworkers regionally in the Yakima Valley, but with implications across the United States. Indeed, I show how migrant farmworkers transformed the airwaves through Chicana/o programming and a community-based media production style that intentionally made radio shows for Spanish-dominant and bilingual Mexican American and Chicana/o audiences. I reconceptualize and question the public broadcasting time line by centering the experiences of Chicana and Chicano community radio broadcasters rather than always beginning linearly with the founding of National Public Radio and the public broadcasting industry in the late 1960s and early 1970s.

Chapter 1, "The Roots of Radio Cadena: Chicana/o Community Radio Formations in the Pacific Northwest," begins my examination of the social, political, and cultural forces behind the emergence of public broadcasting, starting with the passage of the Public Broadcasting Act of 1967 and its effects on the formation of Chicano public radio in the United States. I situate community-based radio technologies within broader sociopolitical and feminist contexts by detailing the activism, legislation, and infrastructure implicated in the making of Chicano public broadcasting. The civil rights era ushered unprecedented shifts in media landscapes, including an increase of ethnic and linguistic cultural productions in film, television, newspapers, print media, and radio broadcasting. The first chapter reframes social movement historiography to include the rise of alternative public broadcasting networks as constitutive of Chicana/o and feminist activism while historically contextualizing the ideologies that fueled this media reform. An in-depth analysis of Radio Cadena's origins and early years are placed within a sociocultural context that reveal how migration, social movement activism, and community radio production converged at this community radio station. Radio Cadena's founders and early radio broadcasters came from migrant farmworker families who were already involved in some form of social justice work and deeply believed in the power of community-driven radio production, which influenced how they engaged in this work, particularly by making community building central to KDNA's cultural work.

Chapter 2, "Brotando del Silencio (Emerging from Silence): Chicana Radio Praxis in Community Public Broadcasting," zeroes in on the tactics and strategies developed through a Chicana radio praxis at Radio Cadena, through the lived experiences and radio work of women such as station manager Rosa Ramón, producer Estella Del Villar, and news director Bernice Zuniga who produced programs like *Mujer*, which broadcasted news stories, music, and informative programming by and for Mexicanas, Tejanas, and Chicanas. The labor involved in creating women-centered productions demonstrates how Radio Cadena's day-to-day activities infused the station with burgeoning feminist radio practices that relied on Chicana feminist forms of grassroots leadership.[67] Engaging in a feminist analysis of community radio production that centers on KDNA's women broadcasters, who embodied writer, creator, producer, and voice on the public airwaves, amplifies community radio's legacy in crafting a public voice for newly politicized Chicanas and Chicanos while articulating on-air Chicana feminist consciousness.

Chapter 3, "Radio Rasquache: DIY Community Radio Programming Aesthetics," explores how Chicana radio praxis tactics are taken up by contemporary Chicana and Latina community radio and podcast producers, even when they don't know the history of Chicana broadcasters, because the conditions and structures that call us to produce are similar: bring information, alternative epistemologies, and entertainment to people who are not included in mainstream media. Chicana radio praxis appears in health programming aimed at migrant farmworkers as Chicana and Chicano broadcasters drafted with care and sensitivity in accessible Spanish a radio script about migrant farmworkers and their experiences with HIV/AIDS in the radionovela *Tres Hombres Sin Fronteras.* Here, I also extend the notion of Chicana radio praxis and feminista frequencies to my own work in community media via Soul Rebel Radio. I also contend with these questions: How is Chicana radio praxis present in contemporary community radio productions? How are feminista frequencies still heard today? The tools and production tactics developed by Chicana radio broadcasters are heard in podcasts by current Chicana, Latina, queer, and femme-identified people producing podcasts tuned to their unique languages, dialects, and aesthetics. The autoethnographic analysis in this chapter delves into my own experiences in community-based collective radio practices in order to illuminate linkages to historical Chicano community broadcasting discussed in chapters 1 and 2, thereby demonstrating the lasting legacy of Chicana/o community radio and its connections to contemporary media. I argue that Chicano community radio like KDNA and newer forms of community media like Soul Rebel Radio are deeply rooted in the visual and sonic traditions of Chicano cultural productions in the United States that sustain a rich archive of visual art, print culture, music, film, and radio and links to other forms of Chicana/o *rasquache* aesthetics. Rather than analyzing Chicano community radio as historical and temporally fixed in the 1970s and 1980s, I see and hear these broadcasts along a continuum of Chicana/o artistic expression that leverages working-class Mexican and Chicana/o cultural practices and aesthetics.

In the epilogue, "Channeling Chicana Radio Praxis Today," I reflect on Chicana radio praxis as a methodology and critical intervention in the documentation and preservation of Chicano community radio. The work of radio and its transmission through frequencies shapes my discussion of Spanish-language programming throughout this book. One of the many reasons radio presents a challenge for researchers is its ubiquity in our everyday lives. Radio is everywhere: in our cars, in restaurant kitchens, and in the fields, radio can be heard blaring. However, this book zeroes in on the process of getting a radio station on air, from application to construction to first broadcast, the people that made this happen, and the unique and trailblazing programming, and how women are at the center of all of this. I elevate women, raise the volume on their work and activism in radio broadcasting, without denying that the larger story involves men and other folks, but I engage with women's radio broadcasting trajectories beginning in the 1970s in the Pacific Northwest corner of the United States. It was in a small rural town in Granger, Washington, that Mexicanas and Chicanas raised their voices, stepped up to the mic, and recorded radio programs that mattered to them, which is *herstory* that inspires our work in media and representation today.

CHAPTER 1

THE ROOTS OF RADIO CADENA

CHICANA/O COMMUNITY FORMATIONS IN THE PACIFIC NORTHWEST

THE SUN SHINES BRIGHT BEHIND A FAMILY PILED IN A STATION wagon with their belongings strapped to the top of the car in a crate branded KDNA 91.9 FM. The license plate visually gestures to the migration of Tejana/os from South Texas's Rio Grande Valley to Washington's Yakima Valley. The family could very well be in the midst of toiling and traveling in traditional migratory routes through Illinois, Michigan, Indiana, Iowa, and Montana.[1] A Spanish *bienvenidos* (welcome) sign directs the Texas natives in a familiar language. The radio program guide—a summary of the programming and an update of current happenings at the station—created by Radio Cadena producers is hand-drawn within a framework that calls out Southwest border culture. The program guide cover displays KDNA as the sun illuminating the path and assisting migrants in their navigation of new spaces across the Pacific Northwest. The young girl in the car on the 1980 program guide cover confirms that migration was a gendered phenomenon and exemplifies Chicana radio praxis at work by visually indexing a historical moment when the migration of male *braceros* (guest workers) and Chicanos shifted to include more women and children into the migrant stream. Program guides indexed entire days with programming catering specifically to the growing Chicana/o community of the Yakima Valley.

KDNA's unique locally produced programming encouraged listeners to learn about migrant education programs and social services on shows like *Mujer (Woman)*, get the latest news on *Noticias Radio Cadena* (*Radio Cadena News*), and groove to *Caravana Musical* (*Musical Caravan*), while it also included programs for children like *El Jardín de los Niños* (*Kindergarten*). While commercial radio allowed only blocks of airtime for Spanish-language or "ethnic programs" along with format radio, which dominated the soundscape in FM broadcasting, community radio broke free from programming restrictions. On commercial radio, "format" became the standard for programming by the late 1950s, which means that "some linguistic minority programming risked being sidelined," as scholar Donald Browne explains. He continues, "Most format stations sought to maintain uniformity of program type throughout their schedules, making it awkward to insert 15-, 30-, or 60-minute program in 'foreign' languages that often had very different content."[2] Radio scholar Bob Lochte reminds us, "The format is the programming strategy designed to deliver the target audience, and only the target audience, throughout the program day."[3] Indeed, most format radio did not want to make room for "other" audiences outside of their target listeners, which often translated to English-dominant audiences. On the other hand, the free-form format like the one at KDNA catered programming to Spanish-speaking farmworker audiences that did not deem their language foreign, but another expression of a bilingual and bicultural Mexican American experience. In fact, programmers changed the start time of programming in the spring to accommodate farmworkers' shifting schedules during the harvest season and included select English music shows and programs like *Sketches of Jazz and Blues*. The community radio format allowed for an exploration of new ways to make media and introduced programming never before heard on the airwaves.

The 1980 *Radio KDNA Program Guide* "Ondas en Español de Primavera" ("Springtime Spanish Airwaves") visually cements many of KDNA's unique characteristics as an emergent Chicana/o-controlled community radio station that served the Yakima Valley's Spanish-dominant migrant farmworkers. According to Dolores Inés Casillas, Spanish-language radio broadcasts function as "acoustic allies" for Latino communities in the United States by "airing advocacy-oriented announcements, popular music, and sounds of Latina America to Spanish-dominant listeners."[4] In few words, but through important visual cues, KDNA's radio broadcasters—community organizers and social activists involved in the Chicano movement in the Pacific Northwest—used the program guide cover as a calling card to Spanish-dominant listeners, inviting them to sonically build community through and with Radio Cadena. In turn, farmworkers harnessed the airwaves as a dialogic community-building space where the Yakima Valley's Mexican American community—a mix of US-born Chicana/os, Mexican immigrants,

and a strong influx of Tejana/o migrants—found, in an often discriminatory and hostile space, sonic refuge on the 91.9 FM dial.

The wellspring of Spanish-language community radio lies in the agricultural heartland of the Yakima Valley in Washington State, and a distinct
Chicana radio praxis evolved at KDNA in the 1970s. Radio is an important
cultural institution that helped Chicanas/os and Mexicanos in the Pacific
Northwest navigate power structures and strengthen their social and cultural
capital, despite not having substantive economic or political power during
this time. Their cultural citizenship, called out by Radio Cadena through a
campesino identity that unified Mexicans and Mexican Americans, was central to programming at KDNA as well as at Chicano public radio stations
across the country.[5] This *campesino* identity—signified in the station's logo
of a farmworker—deliberately included women in how they were addressed
and who was addressing them. Radio Cadena belongs to the same "techno-
cultures" Curtis Marez explores in *Farm Worker Futurism: Speculative
Technologies of Resistance,* which proves how "Mexican migrant workers
have taken up technology and formed complex techno-cultures . . . in ways
largely invisible to many contemporary U.S. Americans."[6] Program
guides—informational pamphlets that, in addition to the programming
schedule, advertised local businesses like Rosario's Bakery—made it a point
to call out to farmworker listeners: "Important national and world-wide
events have continued to have a significant impact on those who grow and
harvest the food we eat. Radio Cadena's daily programming will include
valuable information and significant features of interest to all consumers."[7]
By inviting women farmworkers into the radio station through a job skills
training program in radio production, KDNA further contributed to the
development of the station's Chicana radio praxis by providing farmworkers like María Estela Rebollosa and Celia Prieto (discussed in chapter 2)
with employment outside of the fields.

Chicana/o activists in the Yakima Valley were mindful of radio's accessibility and its ability to cross communication barriers by sonically reaching
newly formed Chicana/o farmworker communities across Washington.
These activists created a community-based broadcasting system through
which the valley's Chicanas/os could circulate culturally relevant news and
music as well as resources to combat institutional barriers and discriminatory practices in the region. Radio Cadena's uniquely farmworker-centered
radio production processes show how Chicano movement activism fueled
community radio programming—and, indeed, the very way radio was produced: collectively, collaboratively, and engaging the everyday lived

experiences of marginalized farmworkers. As women further solidified their central role in farm labor, KDNA was there to direct them to social services, educational opportunities, employment, and health and well-being through radio programming and community events like health fairs and *tardeadas*. Many of the programs and visual literature like *fotonovelas* (graphic novels or photographs with short text captions) that I discuss in chapter 3 presented women as central participants in sexual health activism, displaying Chicana radio praxis at work in the community as well as health advocacy and education.

Radio Cadena's cultural work in the Pacific Northwest and the efforts spearheaded by Chicana/o community activists showcase an investment in permeating community radio with Spanish-language programming for migrant farmworkers. They created dynamic, locally produced public-affairs and educational radio shows about nutrition, employment, education, government, arts, and culture with the goal of building community and making farmworkers' lives better. Radio Cadena's origins and early years existed within a sociocultural context that reveals the ways migration, social-movement activism (the Chicano movement and women's activism), and community radio production converged at KDNA. That is to say, Radio Cadena's story is incomplete without an amplified discussion of the social, political, geographic, and cultural conditions influencing all aspects of the radio production process—from the producers themselves to how and why they created the content they did. The fact that Radio Cadena's founders and early radio broadcasters came from migrant farmworker families, were already involved in some form of social-justice work, and deeply believed in the power of community-driven radio production influenced how they engaged in this work, particularly by making community-building central in establishing KDNA's cultural work and putting women at the center of this work.

The emergence of a Chicana radio praxis at Radio Cadena is best understood in the context of various social movement and public broadcasting media histories. First, Radio Cadena exists because of migration to Central and Eastern Washington and social-movement organizing of Chicanas/os in the Pacific Northwest, many with familial and cultural roots in South Texas.[8] Their activism fueled regional social movements that fought against the plight of working-class communities, and it coincided with the rise of community-based public broadcasting made possible partly with the passing of the 1967 Public Broadcasting Act, which Washington State Senator Warren Magnuson had a hand in crafting.[9] In the Pacific Northwest, the viability of broadcasting Spanish-language radio content for eighteen hours a day, seven days a week, was facilitated by the presence of migrant farmworker families of Mexican descent who began settling in the Pacific Northwest as early as the late 1940s and 1950s.[10] Innovators of community radio technologies were rooted in a population of migrant farmworkers comprised of US citizens of Mexican descent and undocumented immigrant workers, many of whom were regionally tied to South Texas and the Rio Grande Valley.

This newly formed Chicana/o community, desperate for Spanish-language media, inspired activists to create a community-based broadcasting system through which the Yakima Valley's Chicanas/os could circulate culturally relevant news and music as well as provide tools to combat sexism, institutional barriers, and discriminatory practices in the region. At the same time that Chicano movement activists in the Yakima Valley decried poor working conditions, discriminatory educational practices, and the general lack of resources for Spanish-speaking communities, a new model of community broadcasting was developing across the United States. An examination of Chicana/o community formations in the Pacific Northwest requires an understanding of the existing systems of power and oppression within which Chicanas/os labored. How did Radio Cadena do this on air, through their programming and community-based outreach?

Dubbed by locals as *la voz del campesino* (the voice of the farmworker), Radio Cadena exemplifies the relationship between the political economics of agribusiness systems that called many Texas Mexican farmworkers to the Yakima Valley fields and the subsequent community formations that hinged upon Chicana/o political, familial, and cultural life. Agribusinesses exploited Mexican and Tejana/o farmworkers, forcing them to work under poor conditions and live in subpar housing. Chicana/o community activists created a radio station that addressed the needs of the rural communities, which were mainly farmworkers laboring in a pro-agribusiness structure.[11] Serving as a sounding board and public voice for farmworkers, Radio Cadena's pro-labor and pro-worker orientation inadvertently fueled an existing tension between farmworkers and agribusiness. Indeed, KDNA's media strategy changed the physical and aural landscape for Chicanas/os in the Yakima Valley through the production of community media aimed at rural farmworkers. Moreover, KDNA is a sonic record of the historical conditions that resulted from the exploitative labor practices of agribusinesses like Crewport and Tandem in the Yakima Valley, as well as the Chicana/o social-movement activism in the region that worked to end this exploitation.

MIGRATIONS TO THE PACIFIC NORTHWEST

The Pacific Northwest is not often considered a bastion for Latina/o communities, with its lush greenery, breathtaking landscapes, and gloomy gray weather in places like Seattle and Portland, and with the overall climate being much colder year-round. Yet the presence of Mexican and Chicano communities in the Pacific Northwest—comprised of Idaho, Oregon, and Washington—dates back to the 1800s.[12] This first phase of migration to the region resulted from cattle ranching, trade transportation, mining, and other activities pertaining to the development and settlement of the Northwest. Scholars have also documented the Spanish presence in the Pacific Northwest dating back to the mid-1700s, which predates the Lewis and Clark Expedition to the region.[13] While the presence of Chicana/o communities in the Pacific Northwest is often forgotten within a Southwest-dominant borderland that geographically constrains Mexican Americans to the Southwest, their internal migration to the Pacific Northwest and the Midwest is documented in scholarly works by Chicana/o historians Antonia Castañeda, Erasmo Gamboa, Jerry García and Gilberto García, Yolanda Alaniz and Megan Cornish, Theresa Delgadillo, and Mario J. Sifuentez, among others.[14]

In the early decades of the twentieth century, the Yakima Valley produced highly specialized and labor-intensive crops that demanded seasonal labor. The eight months needed to properly thin and weed sugar beets, for example, required backbreaking labor with an added expectation that workers would arrive early enough for spring thinning and return for the fall harvest.[15] The vehicle's Texas license plate on the cover of the 1980 *Radio KDNA Program Guide* "Ondas en Español de Primavera" ("Springtime Spanish Airwaves") illustrates that many of the families that came to work in the Pacific Northwest began their migration in Texas. As Jerry García notes, "Oral interviews conducted . . . in Quincy have revealed that the Chicano pioneers of the community were not recent immigrants from México, but U.S. citizens of Mexican descent who followed long established migratory routes north out of the Southwest. The majority of Chicanos arriving in Quincy during the late 1940s and early 1950s originated from Texas, in particular the Rio Grande Valley in South Texas."[16]

During World War II, *braceros* (male guest workers) and Chicano laborers from the Southwest were actively recruited to the Pacific Northwest to address increased labor shortages in areas like the agricultural sector.[17] Irrigation projects in the Yakima Valley during this time also increased the viability and availability of land for the cultivation of nonmechanized crops like hops, asparagus, apples, and sugar beets. In the Pacific Northwest, companies such as the Amalgamated Sugar Company and the Utah and Idaho Sugar Company offered paid labor opportunities to a mostly Mexican-immigrant male population.[18] The Bracero Program (1942–64) was a bilateral agreement between the United States and Mexico regarding temporary guest workers that brought nearly 4.6 million Mexican workers, *braceros*, to fields and factories across the United States.[19] Under the Bracero Program, farmers were responsible for providing transportation, housing, and food as well as paying for work permits. Mexican and Tejana/o migration to the Pacific Northwest increased after 1948 as the agricultural industry enlisted fewer Mexican *braceros* and turned to the recruitment of Mexican Americans from the Southwest. But growers in the Pacific Northwest eventually realized that the costs to recruit, transport, house, and feed *braceros*—even for the poor housing and working conditions the growers provided—could be dramatically lowered if they shifted from Mexican nationals to Mexican American migrant workers and their families. While farmers had relied on *braceros* to address labor shortages during and after World War II, starting in the 1950s agribusinesses preferred to hire entire Chicano migrant families, many of whom followed the various migratory streams from Texas, Colorado, and Wyoming.[20] Historian Erasmo Gamboa explains, "It was not by chance that farmers sought Chicano laborers. These migrants, mostly families, had clear advantages over braceros . . . they offered farmers the security of a stable labor force and freed them from the troublesome annual practice of contracting Mexican nationals."[21] The family on the *Radio KDNA Program Guide* shown packed in the car signals this very phenomenon.

As the bodies of labor changed from predominantly male Mexican migrants to family units, men, women, and children labored alongside one another performing the same type of stoop labor. Once the harvest was over, these families were expected to go back "home." As Ricardo García recalls, "After the final apple harvest, the agricultural industry made sure that these Texas farmworkers would go back to their state. They [agribusinesses] would throw big parties and would say 'thank you for helping us with the harvest, we'll see you next year. Goodbye.'"[22] The behavior displayed by growers deemed farmworkers as expendable and disposable after the harvest was over. Yet Radio Cadena, with its uplifting cultural programming and community gatherings at the radio station, created a welcoming environment for these families.

The migration of Chicanas in the Pacific Northwest, while not comparable to the number of Chicanos in the region, has been documented in oral histories. For example, Chicanas in Idaho were part of *Voces Hispanas* (Hispanic Voices), an Idaho Hispanic Oral History Project, which documented their lived experiences in the region.[23] Scholars like Jerry García and Dora Sanchez Treviño, Jerry García and Gilberto García, and Yolanda Alaniz have used familial migration narratives to uncover the histories of Chicana/o communities in the Pacific Northwest.[24] Renowned Chicana historian Antonia Castañeda revives histories of Chicana/o migration to the Pacific Northwest through her family's personal migration narrative, centering "gendered, racialized, sexualized and historicized working-class Chicana bodies and the transregional migration of farmworkers from Texas to Washington state during the mid-twentieth century."[25] As Castañeda argues, the internal migration of Chicanas from Texas to Washington "is an outgrowth of the consolidation of U.S. military conquest, of capitalist development, and of state and national politics in the western half of the United States and must be understood within that context. It cannot be understood within a strictly regional context."[26]

Throughout the 1950s, families worked the fields of Eastern Washington for five to six months picking asparagus and then returned to Texas by way of California, where they also found seasonal work.[27] Farmers and public entities strategically recruited workers to Eastern Washington by implementing advertising campaigns in places like Texas and California. Spanish-language ads aired on radio programs, in newspapers, and in posters at communal spaces like dance halls and stores.[28] Many *enganchados* (contract laborers) traveled as family units because they needed the entire family, including children, to work in order to earn enough money to survive. For instance, Castañeda writes, "The Pérez family, like all migrant farmworker families, was an economic unit. No matter how big or how little, everyone's labor, including that of pregnant women and nursing mothers, was necessary to the family's survival."[29]

Once in the Northwest, Chicana and Chicano workers were instrumental in the economic development of the Columbia Basin. Chicanas, who comprised a large portion of the workforce, helped build and shape many agricultural industries at various scales of production, from harvest to packing and canning. Chicano historian Jerry García, in his oral history interview with his mother, Dora Sánchez Treviño, highlights the gender segmentation and discrimination in the paid labor force:

When Dora was growing up and migrating from state to state with her extended family, she indicated that men and women worked side by side doing the same type of work. It appears that while women worked in the fields with men, women did the same work as men and were paid on an equal basis, resulting in an environment with little tension between workers. However, in the more structured environment of the warehouses, where positions were filled based on gender, foremen exhibited a number of unfair practices, and Chicanas were relegated to the lowest-paying work.[30]

García notes that women were not paid the same wages as men in warehouses and packing sheds. As his mother recounts, "In the potato sheds the women were always put [to work] on the conveyor belts to sort the potatoes, and it was constant and rapid work. And the men never worked on the belts but would be paid between ten and twenty-five cents more an hour. . . . Women rarely received any breaks during the day, and the less pay was what bothered me."[31] It is in this context that women figured into the equation as paid and unpaid workers.

Once women and children joined men in the fields, education factored in as a reason to establish roots in the Pacific Northwest. Families began to settle across the Yakima Valley in places like Granger, Sunnyside, and Toppenish to provide more educational stability for their children in addition to the availability of year-round employment. Community activist and KDNA volunteer Tomás Villanueva (who also founded the Farm Worker Clinic) explains that his family settled in Toppenish because his parents wanted their children to get an education. "They were very concerned, especially for my younger sister Delfina and brother Vicente," Villanueva recalls; "for three years, they had been going to first grade in school and never got out of first grade. So my dad decided, 'Well, we have to settle someplace, so it may as well be here.' So we settled in Toppenish in 1958."[32] Similarly, Rosa Ramón's family decided to make their home in Sunnyside, Washington, which offered stability and better educational opportunities.

The presence of Chicanas/os in the Pacific Northwest grows from a larger historical contextualization within national and transnational narratives of migration, class, gender, race, and sexuality. As Castañeda also reminds us, "The first Mexican-descent workers to migrate internally within the United States as mobile seasonal laborers were neither foreigners nor Mexican immigrants. They were Californianos, Tejanos, Nuevo Mexicanos, and native-born U.S. citizens made exiles, aliens, and foreigners in their native land."[33] Indeed, it is critical to keep in mind that the internal migration of Mexican-descent peoples within the United States was not willful travel but forced displacement that turned Chicana/o US citizens into outsiders and eradicated any claims they had to land or rights in a territory that was now foreign to them. Castañeda's Chicana feminist historicization of Chicana migration to the Pacific Northwest is a key intervention into existing literature that privileges male narratives of migration and labor. As will be shown, farmworker women went on to mitigate and sonically represent this displacement through the creation of community-based radio.

Radio Cadena's broadcasts convened a Spanish-language-dominant audience that made the Pacific Northwest their home. In the decade of KDNA's founding, from 1970 to 1980, the presence of Chicana/o residents in Yakima County rose 74.9 percent, from 14,556 in 1970 to 25,455 in 1980.[34] The growing presence of Chicanas/os in rural Washington towns included areas that had the highest concentration of these communities: Mabton (65.4 percent of the population), Granger (54.3 percent), Wapato (47 percent), Toppenish (43 percent), Sunnyside (36 percent), and Pasco (20 percent)—all towns within KDNA's range of transmission. Migrant families were often mixed status, meaning some members of the family were US citizens and others were Mexican nationals, even among children.

The treatment of farmworkers activated the community to fight for better conditions and became the grounds on which many of KDNA's founders first began organizing. Farmworker organizing in the Pacific Northwest was fashioned through a variety of grassroots organizations and student activist groups, including the United Farm Worker Cooperative (UFW Co-op), Northwest Rural Opportunities (NRO), the Washington State Commission on Mexican American Affairs, United Mexican American Students (UMAS), and the Brown Berets.[35] In 1969 César Chávez visited Granger, Washington, where he spoke to approximately 800 Chicanas/os at a local school, and some of KDNA's founders were in attendance, which motivated their own farmworker organizing.[36] He would later visit Radio Cadena in 1983, which inspired him to start the UFW's own network of Spanish-language radio stations, the Radio Campesina Network.[37]

As KDNA considered the best way to reach farmworker communities, radio emerged as the clear front runner. In farmworker rural communities, print media was not as effective or accessible as radio. Illiteracy, along with long work hours, meant that farmworkers were unlikely to come home to read a newspaper. Thus, Chicana/o activists in rural areas opted for radio over other visual media like newspapers or television, though this isn't to say that there weren't any Chicano-owned media like newspapers or public television programs. Radio Cadena's producers chose to harness the potential of community radio to reach audiences that commercial radio often forgot or excluded.

ACTIVIST ORIGINS

Chicana and Chicano community activists crossed over into the realm of community radio production with the political consciousness they cultivated in Chicano and women's-movement organizing. Radio Cadena founders Rosa Ramón and Ricardo García are in many ways emblematic of this history of Chicana/o migration from the Southwest to the Pacific Northwest. Ramón's family's migration echoes the process by which many Mexican American, and specifically Tejano, families traveled from the Southwest to the Northwest in search of jobs, many ending up in the Yakima Valley to cultivate hops, apples, and asparagus, among other crops. Ramón's family traveled from Texas through Arizona and California before settling down in Eastern Washington, where her family purchased a small farm in 1951. There was already a small community of Chicanas/os, primarily Mexican Americans and Tejanos, who were moving to the Yakima Valley when Ramón's family arrived. "We grew up on a farm where we had animals," Ramón recalls; "we had horses, pigs, and chickens—and we grew our own vegetables and canned our own food because we were such a large family. That was how you supported a family of ten back then. You don't have a lot of money, but you do grow your own crops and can your own food and raise your own animals."[38]

Although the small community where Ramón grew up was mostly comprised of Tejano families, she experienced and witnessed racism and discrimination, especially at school, where she was reprimanded for speaking Spanish and witnessed students being mocked for eating tacos instead of bologna sandwiches. Ramón was only one of eight Latinos to graduate from Grandview High School in the mid-1960s. She recalls, "There were some experiences that were a little bit painful that you don't forget, like playing in the school grounds and getting so excited that you start speaking Spanish and then having a teacher grab you by the arm and hit you with a book, telling you to stop speaking that gibberish because that's not the language that you should be speaking."[39]

Ramón's experiences are just one example of the way institutional racism operated in the Yakima Valley. While Mexican American students may have predominated, they were economically and culturally relegated to a subordinate status. In his oral history interview with his mother, Dora Sánchez Treviño, Pacific Northwest scholar and historian Jerry García documents these challenges: "The assumption was made that any new Mexican student was here for the harvest. I remember one of my Anglo teachers telling me, 'Oh, you are here for the harvest and the weeding.' At that time, I had no idea what she was talking about, and I looked at her puzzled. I thought that maybe I should answer yes. From that time on I began to get the feeling that maybe I should answer yes to the things they wanted to hear."[40] For people of a newly formed Chicana/o community in a predominantly white region, discriminatory experiences like these served as a catalyst for the type of activism they would later engage in with the Chicano movement of the Pacific Northwest.

Ramón's community work began shortly after she graduated from high school. Her postgraduation choices were limited due to financial constraints— her family could not economically support her collegiate aspirations—as well as employment discrimination. For instance, when Ramón applied for an entry-level clerical job, she noticed her résumé in the trash as she walked out the door. These early memories of marginalization served as an impetus for Ramón to work in nonprofits that benefitted her community. At the age of nineteen, Ramón began working with War on Poverty programs to inform farmworker families about early-childhood education programs. This experience trained her to work with the Washington State Commission on Mexican American Affairs (newly established in 1971) and Northwest Rural Opportunities (NRO), a community-based organization set up in 1968 to provide services to seasonal and migrant farmworkers in Washington State.

The War on Poverty programs were a catalyst for many Yakima Valley Chicanas/os to get involved in political organizing and community-based organizations. Chicanas in Quincy, Washington, for instance, "benefited from the Great Society programs implemented by the Johnson administration in the 1960s. Programs such as the Migrant Day Care Center, the Quincy Community Center, the Grant County Community Action Council, and Northwest Rural Opportunities were all funded by the War on Poverty programs. Dora, . . . along with many others, received valuable training and leadership experience during this time period."[41] Many organizations that emerged in Washington during this time sought ways to inform workers of their rights and create better working conditions for the backbreaking stoop labor in the Yakima Valley. In 1974 Ramón became assistant director of the Parent and Child Center in Grandview, Washington, that formed part of NRO's community social services programs. Her commitment to working in her community, combined with her growing interest in communication technologies, would later converge at Radio Cadena. Her experiences proved to be beneficial on-the-ground training for navigating bureaucratic structures, a skill she would later utilize to navigate the quagmire of applying for a broadcasting license.

While she was at NRO, Ramón met Ricardo García, the director of the organization at the time. Like Ramón, García had gained insights from his life experiences that he applied to his work as an organizer and that would later align with Radio Cadena's goal of being *la voz del campesino*. Born in San Diego, Texas, Ricardo Romano García was only two and a half years old when his father died from tuberculosis, after which he was raised by his mother. Relegated to what he describes as "second-class citizen status" after his father's death, which left his mother to seek low-wage work, García witnessed the structural inequities and discrimination that Tejanas/os were forced to contend with daily. His mother worked day and night for meager wages that kept their household in a cycle of poverty and food scarcity. García explains that his gender consciousness stemmed from his mother and is perhaps also based on observing gender roles as a child:

> The whole root of it comes from sensitivity to my mother and aunts, who were brilliant women in their own way but never had a chance to develop. They didn't go to school. My grandmother also raised them after her husband, Manuel Romano, died from tuberculosis. My father died of tuberculosis. My grandmother had to raise a family of eight. They were picking cotton all over the area and that was very hard work. They missed out unfairly. They also had husbands who drank and treated them harsh, to say the least. They were good men. They were providers, but they would go to San Diego to the cantinas and drink. It was a hard life for them. I was raised by women and that's where my sensitivity comes from.[42]

What García refers to as "sensitivity" is an awareness of the intersectional conditions that created different challenges for Mexican women. García's early childhood experiences with poverty, gender inequality, and social injustice would no doubt prove influential to his community activism in the Pacific Northwest and, in particular, his support of strategic and intentional inclusion of women in Radio Cadena's founding and operations.

After graduating high school, García joined the US Army, which took him to California, South Korea, Washington State, and, finally, the Yakima Valley, where he settled down and became active in the Chicano movement. After training for a week in California with César Chávez, García worked with the United Farm Workers Organizing Committee in Washington to teach farmworkers about their right to unionize to combat low wages and poor working conditions.[43] With most of the migrant Chicana/o and Mexicano population, including García, settling in the eastern part of Washington State during the 1950s and 1960s the Chicano movement in the Pacific Northwest coalesced around rural farmworker activism. Indeed, the migration of Chicana/o communities to the Pacific Northwest and the dismal working conditions they were subjected to fueled the Chicano movement in this region. A sampling of community organizations founded during the late 1960s through the 1970s illustrates the focus on farmworker and labor organizing through such nonprofit organizations sprouting up across the Pacific Northwest as United Farm Workers Cooperative (founded in 1967), Northwest Rural Opportunities (started in 1968), and the Washington State Commission on Mexican American Affairs (established in 1971). Tomás Villanueva, who volunteered at Radio Cadena in the early days, had earlier established the United Farm Workers Cooperative in Toppenish. As he describes it, "The Co-op sold food at reduced prices and was a center of the Chicana/o movement in the valley for several years. It pressed for enforcement of health regulations in labor camps, pushed for farmworker coverage under industrial insurance, and, with other groups, forced the state to drop its English literacy requirements for voters."[44] Social movements in the Yakima Valley, particularly efforts to improve the working and living conditions for farmworkers, provided a rich foundation for the emergence of Radio Cadena.

García served as the first executive director for the Washington State Commission on Mexican American Affairs, which Governor Daniel Evans established in 1971 to improve public-policy development and access to government services for the Mexican American community. García served as executive director for the commission from 1971 to 1974. His tenure ended when the commission's board of directors fired him because they felt that his Chicano farmworker activism was too radical. That is when he became director of NRO, where he met with other directors of farmworker programs in Idaho and Oregon and was tasked with finding ways of broadcasting information in Spanish. Chicana/o activists searching for a means to reach farmworkers in the Yakima Valley through the radio airwaves implemented a tactic familiar in Spanish-language broadcasting: the purchasing of airtime to broadcast specific content. García recalls of his early experiences as a radio broker, "That's my first experience with radio. We paid for a half-hour program out of KARY out of Prosser, and this was a weekly Spanish-language weekend programming. And we would talk about César Chévez and scabs, and we would talk about farmworkers that were being manipulated by their employers. Word of this content got to the governor and next time he appointed commissioners, he made sure that he appointed some that were conservative and were willing to come back and terminate my employment, and that happened. But we kept going."[45] García continued his work with NRO, and during a presentation he gave to Chicano students at Western Washington University, García met two future KDNA cofounders, Daniel Robleski (also known as Dan Roble) and Julio César Guerrero.

In 1975 Roble and Guerrero came to Washington seeking to replicate a model of radio production they had implemented in Lansing, Michigan: training migrant farmworker youth to produce radio. The station's only woman cofounder, Rosa Ramón, explains the origins of farmworker-centered radio: "There was a group that was interested in trying to come up with a way to provide more information to the Latino community, and specifically the farmworker community in the Yakima Valley. I got involved as a volunteer, and it so happened that there were two gentlemen that moved from the state of Michigan. They came from Lansing where they had worked on a radio project with farmworkers. They were looking to find someone that would have an interest to continue to do that same kind of work here."[46] Indeed, farmworker activism was a cornerstone of KDNA's formation, leaving a significant imprint on the type of programming elevated at the station.

As this brief history illustrates, in the late 1960s and early 1970s Eastern Washington was buzzing with Chicana/o movement activity, reflecting the social, political, and economic life of a newly established community of Mexican American families who decided to plant roots throughout the Yakima Valley rather than continuing on a well-worn migrant trail. Their history challenges a narrative of emerging after the Chicano movement that was well established in the Southwest. Chicano movement organizing in the Pacific Northwest maps onto time lines from organizing in the Southwest, but also brings another dimension to an understanding of Chicana/o activism. Ramón's and García's experiences, and Radio Cadena's founding, track a different narrative about the Chicano movement that elucidates the organizing in the region while grounding larger movement discourses in a rural setting outside of the Southwest. Many of the organizations that emerged in Washington in that era sought ways to inform workers of their rights and create better working conditions in the Yakima Valley. As KDNA cofounder García explains, "We were right there from the very beginning. And when I say 'we,' there was a group of leadership that emerged that understood why it was important to organize. We understood why it was important to seek political power and representation, which would enhance the efforts of the farmworkers' movement. We knew each other from Yakima City to Prosser to Grandview to the Yakima Valley. Many of us were in contact, organizing boycotts for César Chávez in front of Safeway stores; we were taught by César Chávez the importance of nonviolence."[47]

As they had been for Rosa Ramón, the War on Poverty programs were a catalyst for many Yakima Valley Chicanas/os to get involved in political organizing and community-based organizations. In keeping with this trend, KDNA's women founders and volunteers, already active in social-movement organizing, would step into the roles of radio producer, station manager, and news director, while shaping a feminist consciousness at the station as they developed their own brand of on-air Chicana feminism. Chicana/o community radio broadcasters produced radio programs that sonically conveyed the advocacy work they performed in the community as farmworker organizers, child welfare advocates, and student activists.

The story of Radio Cadena and the Chicana/o radio activists who saw the radical potential in radio provides new frameworks that amplify the sound migrations of Chicana/o media activism and the third spaces and technological tools of the Chicano movement, not just in the Pacific Northwest but throughout the country. Aurally, Radio Cadena became the sounding board for issues confronting migrant Tejana/o and Chicana/o communities of the region. Spatially, the radio station served as a community center where Chicanas/os could turn for information, entertainment, and *convivencia* (intentionally gathering as a community). The political work of Radio Cadena as *la voz del campesino*—a hub for farmworker activism in the Yakima Valley—shifts the historical understanding of the Chicano movement to a site for media activism within a rural context beyond the US Southwest.

AND RADIO . . . AND RADIO . . . AND RADIO . . .
THE PUBLIC BROADCASTING ACT OF 1967

Before Chicana and Chicano media activists began to dream of starting their own community-owned and -run radio stations, the infrastructure for public broadcasting was being set in place. The enactment of the Public Broadcasting Act in 1967 marked a new phase in the national movement for media reform and created the conditions of possibility for Chicano community radio stations to emerge in the 1970s—including KBBF FM, Radio Cadena, and Radio Bilingüe, among other bilingual and Spanish-language noncommercial radio stations. Federal legislative task forces had been appointed to study the benefits of public broadcasting television: in 1965 the Carnegie Corporation of New York convened a fifteen-member panel known as the Carnegie Commission on Educational Television (Carnegie I), which then released a report called *Public Television: A Program for Action* in 1967. This commission popularized the term "public television," and the idea that public broadcasting could be leveraged as an educational tool is no surprise, given that those involved in the commission came from universities and foundations.[48] Parties involved with the drafting of the legislation were excited with the visual medium, and at first the bill did not include radio broadcasting as a service within public broadcasting. Radio was such a last-minute inclusion into the public broadcasting bill that the words "and radio" were taped to it in several places throughout the document.[49]

Supporters of public broadcasting, particularly if it were to be reflective of the cultural diversity in the United States, viewed the role of public radio as contributing to a more diverse and equitable society. Public radio advocates believed that the creation of an equitable society could be based in sound and that people could experience different cultures by hearing "various cultural viewpoints to achieve a broader world view by American society." Bill Siemering, cofounder of National Public Radio (NPR) and creator of the station's flagship program *All Things Considered*, drafted NPR's mission statement after his experiences in a storefront-broadcast facility in Buffalo, New York, in 1963–'64. There, Siemering worked with African American broadcasters who primed him as he drafted NPR's mission statement, which capitalized on radio's unique characteristics as a sound-based medium that could be both "aspirational and practical." At the signing of the public broadcasting legislation, President Lyndon B. Johnson remarked: "I want to create a great network of knowledge, not just a broadcast system, one that employs every means for sending and storing information. Think of the lives that this could change: the student in a small college could tap the resources of a great university. The country doctor could get help from a distant laboratory or teaching hospital. A scholar in Atlanta might draw on a library in New York."[50] There was a creative vision behind public broadcasting as a system or network for knowledge, like the internet is today, and radio would prove to connect communities across the United States.

Early iterations of community radio appeared in listener-supported broadcasts that developed after World War II. The idea of listener-supported radio was championed by Lewis Hill and the Pacifica Network he helped establish in 1946. Based on a philosophy of nonviolence, the pacifists that started the Pacifica Foundation strengthened the ideological backbone behind public grassroots community radio: creative exchange through dialogue facilitated by the radio airwaves.[51] "The Pacifica Foundation," writes radio historian Matthew Lasar, "had its ideological roots in a set of communitarian values drawn from Gandhian pacifism, anarchism, and cooperativism."[52] This pacifism, and belief that radio could function as dialogue, resonated with farmworker organizing tactics, especially those of César Chavez, which influenced Radio Cadena's ideology.

The Public Broadcasting Act was instrumental in creating a funding mechanism for community-based media via the Corporation for Public Broadcasting (CPB) to develop and expand educational broadcasting. As Dolores Inés Casillas argues, "In many ways, the establishment of the CPB made it possible for community groups to hold a government-sponsored entity accountable for issues of employment and representation within public broadcasting."[53] CPB gave radio stations money for training programs, which stations like KDNA would later use to train radio broadcasters and create programming, as Ricardo García explained:

> Where do you find the money to maintain a radio station? We learned about underwriting by belonging to national organizations that were also starting without a lot of concrete base to help community radio. I'm referring to the National Federation of Community Broadcasters. The beginning leadership of NFCB were very, very supportive of what we were doing, and so from that we learned about the importance of complying with the Corporation for Public Broadcasting policies so you can become a station that is eligible for grants that were given out every year to community radio and television. But one of the requirements was that you had to raise an amount, an incredible amount, of money to be eligible to get the CPB grant.[54]

In 1969 the CPB began awarding stations general support grants, later called community service grants,[55] which many Chicano community radio stations received early in their founding. In response to critiques and published reports signaling the lack of diversity in public broadcasting, the CPB launched minority training programs. CPB grants often included money for radio stations to hire and train staff in broadcasting, as well as direct trainings provided by the CPB to radio stations. By the early 1980s, nearly two dozen stations owned by African Americans, Latinos, and Native Americans were receiving annual support grants from CPB.

While the Public Broadcasting Act's charge was to open the airwaves to diverse voices, for its first ten years the CPB supported only a handful of radio stations owned and operated by people of color. The stations that did manage to get off the ground and piece together enough of an operational budget to run a public radio station infused community broadcasting with enthusiastic energy to create programming by, for, and about Chicanas and Chicanos. But throughout the 1970s and into the 1980s, public radio became a battleground for equitable treatment and representation of minoritized groups in public broadcasting.

The critiques of public broadcasting as a predominantly white male cultural institution were recognized and documented by two task forces in the 1970s: the 1975 Task Force on Women in Public Broadcasting and the 1978 Task Force on Minorities in Public Broadcasting, with Dr. Gloria Anderson spearheading both projects.[56] The 1975 *Report of the Task Force on Women in Public Broadcasting* assessed the employment and representation of women in public broadcasting. The 1978 report *A Formula for Change: The Report of the Task Force on Minorities in Public Broadcasting* indexed the roadblocks that hampered the participation of women, African Americans, and Chicanos in public broadcasting. It found that only 11 percent of minority women had participated in technical training.[57] Furthermore, most if not all of the chief engineers in public broadcasting were men, which cast this technical role as male.[58] By 1978, "Congress explicitly charged CPB to take a more aggressive role in encouraging minority ownership of public broadcasting."[59]

These statistics are indicative of the status of the field of public broadcasting, especially the potential challenges women faced in technical positions, which put KDNA and its women staff at the forefront of more equitable conditions in public broadcasting.[60] The task forces did not create Chicano community radio—they provided a funding mechanism for it, but that mechanism was tied to fixed notions of diversity, a reification of "minority programming" that rather than changing the institutional practices that excluded minoritized voices and talents, instead resulted in their codification in special segments and time slots. Changing the institution from the inside out is exactly what Chicanas at community radio stations did by hiring women as producers, making programing for and about women, and building community that recognized the diversity of these communities. KDNA's founding is emblematic of this.

EARLY KDNA PROGRAMMING

Before KDNA was founded, media options for Spanish-speaking Mexicans and Tejanas/os in the Yakima Valley were limited. The Concilio (Council) for the Spanish Speaking was established in Seattle in 1975 with the purpose of uniting all charitable, health, and welfare organizations and groups serving Spanish-speaking communities. Concilio, as it was known, published a news magazine, *La Voz: The News Magazine of the Concilio for the Spanish-Speaking*, which ran an article by Julio César Guerrero and Rosa Ramón titled "Mujeres in Public Radio" (discussed in chapter 2). Organizations across the Yakima Valley, including Northwest Rural Opportunities, where Ricardo García and Rosa Ramón were employed at the time, sought access to the televised airwaves. *La Raza Habla (The People Speak)*, a thirty-minute talk show focused on Chicano issues, aired for twelve to fifteen weeks on KIMA TV, as did a program titled *Chicano '73* that aired on KNDO TV, all in Yakima.[61] However, the high cost of producing television programming prohibited a sustained endeavor to create televised programming for Chicanos in the valley.

Farmworker activism in the Yakima Valley was a driving force for the creation of Radio Cadena. To begin the process of creating a Spanish-language radio station, KDNA's founders formed the Northwest Chicano Radio Network (NCRN). Organized and incorporated as a nonprofit entity in April 1976, NCRN planned to "gather, collect, and disseminate information and data on all affairs pertaining to this regional Chicano community to Spanish-speaking individuals and/or groups, organizations and programs in the Northwest via radio programming and media conferences."[62] NCRN was originally conceived as a tristate radio initiative between Washington, Idaho, and Oregon. The designated tagline for NCRN would be Radio Cadena, which translates as "chain" or "link" in English, signaling how activists imagined radio technologies as a way to link Chicana/o organizers and farmworker communities across these three states in the Pacific Northwest.[63] Unfortunately, the tristate radio model did not materialize as planned, but Ramón, García, and the other cofounders moved forward with creating a radio station in the Yakima Valley. While Radio Cadena cofounders were preparing the application to the Federal Communications Commission (FCC) for a licensing and construction permit, they also began broadcasting Spanish-language radio programming in Seattle at community radio station KRAB 107.7 FM through the use of the station's subsidiary communications authorization (SCA) signal.[64]

KRAB, which operated out of a fire station on Capitol Hill in Seattle, played a vital role in KDNA's founding. *Seattle Magazine* described KRAB in 1964 as an "offbeat little FM station which refuses to take advertising but will happily put on anything else that people care to hear—or to air. Of the four listener-supported stations in the country, it is the only one which is independently owned and operated. Its subscribers pay $12 a year, but KRAB keeps right on running impressive deficits. The advantages of this unique system are obvious, for KRAB is getting more irresistible all the time."[65] The article goes on to give a better understanding of KRAB's value:

> On any given day, people who show up at the studios may include housewives, high school kids, physicians, lawyers and assorted beatniks. Their combined experience in radio amounts to almost nothing, and their social and political opinions, if they happen to have any, are as disparate as their backgrounds. Therein lies the great value of KRAB. It is Seattle's leading medium for the unusual, the offbeat, the unpopular, and—often—the unheard-of. Material for KRAB has to meet only two conditions: it must have inherent quality and it must, by its very nature, be unlikely to get aired by any other radio station.[66]

When Radio Cadena began operating out of KRAB FM in Seattle in 1976, they used the facilities at the old fire station for radio services that supported four objectives: (1) develop and train young Chicanos to gather news and information that related to the Chicano and farmworker community; (2) develop a technical system that was simple and allowed Chicano reporters the opportunity to disseminate their work beyond their local areas; (3) allow Spanish-language radio programs easy access to the reporters and information of Radio Cadena; and (4) allow the greatest number of Chicano listeners the opportunity to hear and better understand the issues that most directly affected them. When community radio producers Julio César Guerrero and Daniel Robleski came to Washington in the mid-1970s, Chicana/o activists in the region were already working to access communication technologies including print media and public access television, and Radio Cadena worked with Northwest Rural Opportunities to train ten farmworker youth in radio production in Lynden, Washington.

Early efforts to build an audience for Radio Cadena's programming included placing special receivers at local Mexican restaurants. Aspirations for a national radio network were printed in the program guide: "Radio Cadena or radio chain is now broadcasting 18 hours each day in Spanish from the KRAB radio station on Capitol Hill. Aimed at King County's approximately 25,000 Chicanos, the subscriber station broadcasts legislative news, educational programs, public affairs, news and music, and the station's originators' dream is that Radio Cadena will become a part of a communications network linking Chicanos across the country."[67]

While Radio Cadena broadcast from Seattle's KRAB FM community radio station, its producers developed an innovative system for coalescing and producing a cutting-edge Spanish-language news production system that was unlike anything heard over the airwaves. What made this Spanish news program unique and ahead of its time was how Radio Cadena leveraged national resources that connected commercial and noncommercial radio stations across the country.[68] Known as the Spanish-Language News Network, this system aurally connected the Pacific Northwest to locations across the United States, including California, Texas, Minnesota, Michigan, Illinois, Colorado, and New Mexico.[69] Spanish-language reporters fed Radio Cadena their news segments through a nationwide incoming toll-free telephone line connected to recording equipment that Spanish-Language News Network producer Julio César Guerrero then produced and transmitted back to the subscribing radio station through the same toll-free phone number. Rosa Ramón explains, "It was a very simple setup: reel to reel and a telephone where news reporters from different radio stations throughout the country would call in and give us radio reports and then we would produce them into one concise segment and then feed them back to the radio stations."[70] Radio Cadena had been attempting to achieve these objectives through the use of a nationwide incoming toll-free line, which included two recorders and eighteen hours of Julio César Guerrero's time daily. Ramón continues, "We receive news reports via the phone lines, research the information, produce informative reports, and feed the information to Spanish-language radio programs through those same toll-free phone lines. The news feed, which are originally written and not translations of wire service news, run from one to two minutes in length."[71] KDNA also shared programming with KBBF in Santa Rosa, California, via the

Spanish-Language News Network.[72] Although the Spanish-Language News Network was operational for only two years while Radio Cadena broadcast from KRAB FM from 1976 to 1978, it facilitated a dialogue between Radio Cadena and other Chicano movement activity across the country through shared news and programming.

However, as Ricardo García recalls, "But this frequency from KRAB was a special frequency that required special receivers, so we purchased about sixty receivers with the idea that if we keep on multiplying these efforts eventually we'd be making a lot of money because we were charging I think it was $50 dollars a month for the use of that radio. It didn't go very far. But by then the idea had come, this radio should be in the Yakima Valley, and that's when we started to work on the application and receiving that permit to construct."[73] As Radio Cadena worked on its application to the Federal Communications Commission (FCC), the cofounders actively engaged various community organizations across the Yakima Valley, including Northwest Rural Opportunities, Foundation for Chicano Education, and the Washington State Commission on Mexican-American Affairs (now the Commission on Hispanic Affairs), which offered staff support and other resources to the burgeoning station. García explains, "A lawyer from Seattle who was an FCC retired judge agreed to help us with the application; he knew the in and out workings of the FCC. He said, 'I'll do it for you for free if you take me to California and meet César Chávez,' and I said, 'Sure.' So Rosa, Dan Roble, myself—we went with him, we took him to California (I can't remember if it was La Paz—it was La Paz), and César was as usual very humble, very welcoming, and the judge . . . took pictures with César and he came back very energized to help with the application, and we got a permit to construct."[74]

On December 19, 1977, the FCC granted the application for a noncommercial public radio station to begin construction. After a year of talks and negotiations with the Yakama Nation, construction of the radio transmitter shack on Ahtanum Ridge began on April 6, 1978. Northwest Rural Opportunities worked with another local nonprofit, the Chicano Education Foundation (CHE), to purchase the abandoned old Highline Hotel in Granger, Washington, known as the Academy from its days as a Seventh-Day Adventist academy; CHE then leased the building to Radio Cadena and the Northwest Chicano Radio Network (NCRN) for one dollar a year. In the old Academy building, Radio Cadena produced local programming, while becoming a central place for information, assistance, entertainment, and *convivencia* for the Yakima Valley's Mexican American and Chicano communities for almost thirty years. The radio station served as a community center and also became a training center that offered courses in radio announcing, upholstery, mechanics, and clerical work under the sponsorship of NRO, managed by Ricardo García.

Radio Cadena's license was later transferred to a new entity, Northwest Communities Education Center (NCEC), which replaced NCRN. NCEC is housed in a multipurpose community center constructed in 2009, which is now Radio Cadena's current home. It boasts not only the radio studio but also facilities for other community-based organizations, as well as meeting spaces for the community.

"RADIO CADENA IS ON THE AIR"

Many Chicano community radio stations used call letters that signified Spanish-language words or slang that signaled a deeper connection rooted in the Spanish language, Spanglish, and Chicana/o subcultures. The Chicana/o community activists in the Yakima Valley who applied for a community radio broadcasting license is one example of a trend around the country by other Latinas/os gaining access to noncommercial airwaves. The fashioning of a station's identity included logos, call letters, and slogans that used Chicana/o coded language, speech, and slang popular at the time, with phrases such as *q'vo* (what's up?). Chicana/o community radio station call letters at Radio Cadena included KDNA, for *cadena* (chain or link), KUVO, for *q'vo* (what's up?), and KRZA, for *raza* (people).

KDNA had been the call letters of a listener-supported station in Saint Louis, Missouri, at 102.5 MHz from 1968 to 1973. While the Midwest radio station's call letters may have signaled something else, the Chicana/o community radio context transforms the call letters to echo Radio Cadena's social and cultural aspects in these spaces of production. Indeed, Radio Cadena cultivated a community radio practice inflected with the intersectional social and political activism that Chicanas and Chicanos engaged with at the time. The call letters represent one manifestation of the station's effort to aesthetically create its own identity as a Chicana/o community radio station.

Radio frequencies carried cultural practices across borders, maintaining a sense of connection to Mexican music, language, and cultural traditions. While the KDNA moniker cleverly captures the radio station's intention of linking farmworkers to each other, the call letters KDNA were not the cofounders' first choice. On July 28, 1976, the Northwest Chicano Radio

Network submitted the construction permit application to the FCC for a noncommercial educational FM radio station called KTZL, for *quetzal*, a colorful long-tailed bird, with operations located at Granger's Academy building. When the application came back with the KTZL FM call letters unavailable, the radio organizers turned to their next choice, KDNA. On December 19, 1979, at noon, the voice of Julio César Guerrero, KDNA cofounder and program manager, welcomed audiences to KDNA, stating, *"Buenos días, Radio Cadena está en el aire"* ("Good morning, Radio Cadena is on the air").

The sounds emanating from KDNA's airwaves carried the political impulses and grassroots activism that originated in a collective agreement that Mexican and Chicana/o farmworkers in the region would benefit from a system of communication. Financing and grants to keep the station operational meant leveraging any and all resources that cultural and social services institutions provided. "In the beginning we were lucky that the Catholic Church, through their national governing board of bishops, they have a foundation, I think it's the Catholic Development Foundation. And they were the very first ones perhaps a foundation that gave out a good-sized grant, about $30,000 a year for three years. That was the commitment, three years at $30,000. Well, that money really went a long way," recalls Ricardo García. Start-up funds from the Campaign for Human Development, along with other resources pooled by community groups, gave KDNA the financial resources to produce programming.

Radio Cadena built a dynamic programming schedule that centered on music, news and public affairs shows, and agricultural programs created especially for local farmworkers. The programming schedule also shifted during the spring to begin at 4:00 a.m. during the weekdays to accommodate farmworkers whose day started earlier during the growing season. News and public affairs programming took on a significantly different sound at KDNA. Not only were these programs written and recorded in Spanish, they also often covered topics not found in mainstream media and were, according to its program guide, "designed to provide the listening audience with a broad and detailed general information of events at a local, state, and national level. This is accomplished by combining the talent and work of the local production staff and news reporters located strategically throughout the Northwest."[75] Perhaps one of the most popular features of KDNA's early programming was a block of Spanish-language music not found on any other radio station in the region at the time. KDNA promised musical offerings: "The most popular items will include folkloric songs, polkas, boleros, rancheras, cumbias, mariachi, traditional Mexican songs, jazz, Chicano pop. Radio KDNA receives its records from over 100 Mexican-Latin-Chicano record companies and will provide a variety of music throughout the broadcast day."[76]

During KDNA's early days, producers strived to air locally produced content and were successful with 95 percent of KDNA's programming. Ricardo García and Rosa Ramón both remember those days as frenetic, given the small staff of five, as García recalls:

> It was hectic, the very early days, because you were there, you had a radio station, you were controlling the radio station. It was a community radio station. It had a board of directors who were Chicanos. It was very hectic because Rosa and her staff were getting into a profession, radio broadcasters, and learning the skills of radio broadcasting as they went along. It also had to face the criticism, the controversy of growers who . . . from the very beginning, I think it was, suspected the radio station . . . was being used for purposes other than entertaining them, purposes other than just playing music for them. That it was a station that was doing a lot of talking, a lot of informing, a lot of meaningful interviews. So those beginning days were hectic for that reason.[77]

Producers needed to fill eighteen hours of programming a day with a variety of material, including music, interviews, informational messages or public service announcements (PSAs), and original programs. Indeed, KDNA's diverse programming transformed radio into a resource for listeners who, as Casillas argues, "are drawn to radio for more than the musical sounds of homelands left behind; from radio they also seek guidance on how to navigate their newfound social and political lives as immigrants. . . . Specifically, these on-air exchanges broadcast listeners' migrant sensibilities and highlight their economic and racialized status in the United States."[78]

Being *la voz del campesino* also meant being a voice against anti-immigrant rhetoric prevalent in the Yakima Valley throughout the 1980s. KDNA's biggest critic in its early years was the Immigration and Naturalization Service (INS), which currently is Immigration and Customs Enforcement (ICE) under the US Department of Homeland Security. The *Yakima Herald-Republic* reported about this in 1984:

> Immigration agents have repeatedly complained about alleged broadcasts alerting illegal aliens when the Border Patrol is operating in the area.

No charges have been filed, but the agency's information was reviewed by the U.S. attorney's office, said Kenneth Langford, chief patrol officer with the Spokane INS office. "It appears there were some infractions" in federal communications law, Langford said. "We've had residents living in that area who have heard the same things and notified us. Of course, it's hard to prove those things unless you have a recording." Ramone [*sic*] said she knows of no official complaints filed against KDNA by the INS. However, the station manager acknowledges relations have been tense between the agencies in recent years, and that immigration officials have refused to talk with KDNA reporters on more than one occasion.[79]

Rosa Ramón was aware that, as she puts it, "immigration wasn't very happy with us at times because we covered stories about immigration and we knew that we were being monitored, right. Because everyone was worried that we were a front for the union and for César Chávez, so we're pretty sure we had a lot of lawyers and immigration people and others monitoring the station in those early days. But of course we were very familiar with FCC rules and regulations."[80] As *la voz del campesino*, the migrant farmworker experience became the anchor for Radio Cadena's audience, programming, and community formation more broadly.

Ramón transitioned out of the role of station manager in 1985, when Ricardo García stepped in to serve as station manager from 1985 until 2008. Amelia Ramón, who was executive director for the Northwest Communities Education Center, the licensee for the Radio Cadena FCC license, began working for Radio Cadena in 1985, initially assisting with administrative tasks.[81] Amelia Ramón, Rosa Ramón's sister, began her early work with KDNA as a volunteer in the 1980s and was instrumental in integrating more health education in KDNA's radio programming as the director for the Northwest Communities Education Center (KDNA's radio licensee) starting in 1985.

RADIO CADENA'S IMPACT ON THE COMMUNITY

KDNA often invited experts to discuss a relevant topic as a way to inform the community and introduce them to experts who had the cultural understanding and community roots to take on difficult topics. For instance, clinical therapist Abel Garza had a weekly call-in counseling program that tackled several taboo mental health and abuse topics prevalent in Latino communities. Ricardo García recalls that the topic of incest within the

Latino community had a great impact. Even after the program aired, many people were calling in to learn more about it and other forms of abuse. For many listeners, particularly women, having a radio program publicly discuss this topic was eye-opening, and for many it was the first time they opened up about their own experiences with incest and abuse. García remembers the phones at KDNA started to ring nonstop after this topic aired and listeners continued calling the station for several weeks. "Women were calling in and sharing not only their experiences of incest at home," García notes, "but what they were going through at home in terms of abuse, harassment by their husbands, who many times were drinking too much and abusing them. They were using radio, through programming that originated at KDNA, that created a change in the way women were thinking."[82] This was the impact of Chicana feminist programming and the work of Chicana radio praxis at KDNA.

Bilingual and Spanish-language community radio stations operated on shoestring budgets and the lack of funding posed challenges, but a station's impact cannot be measured by monetary gains alone. Even with limited funds, Radio Cadena provided its employees with benefits and certainly made an impact on the Chicano community in the region, as Rosa Ramón explains:

> You had a community that started to participate. You had a community that started to settle down, establish roots. That was a big accomplishment of Radio Cadena, convincing our Texas migrant and seasonal farm-workers to establish roots. You had children going to school listening to *El Jardin de los Niños*, but also graduating and going to college, the universities. And several years later coming back and that's what you have right now, you have a lot of the offspring of the first generation of Tex-Mex and later on the immigrant families of the eighties coming back, and they're the teachers, they're the lawyers, they're the doctors, they're the dentists; there's a core of professional, skilled, experienced workforce in the valley, thanks to the development of a community that was listening to Radio Cadena.[83]

Radio fills a void in our knowledge of the everyday life of Chicanas/os in Eastern Washington. KDNA sheds light, opens ears, and amplifies community radio as a place where we hear a distinct form of radio that is informed by the broadcasters, listeners, and community members of an emergent Pacific Northwest Chicana/o public. Everyday life appears in the pages of the program guide, in the programming, and in the *tardeadas* (gatherings) at the radio station for music on Saturday or Sunday afternoons. At KDNA, listener support expanded into new spaces because radio broadcasters engineered ways to engage their audiences face to face through community events, health fairs, and Sunday-afternoon *tardeadas* for workers to enjoy food and music. Ricardo García remembers that the goal was to build community with listeners, not just create individual underwriters to fund the station:

> We created outside the school, we built a *kiosko* and we built a cement round [for] the *kiosko* and it was wide enough for dancing, so we had live groups from the valley coming on Sundays and playing live music and . . . they were fundraising events for the radio. We sold tacos and refreshments and balloons and things like that to raise money. On a good Sunday, we could make a thousand dollars, . . . and people would come and they would dance around the *kiosko* and have a lot of fun, and they would support the radio station in that way. Meanwhile, the Anglo-Saxon community around the school would complain because we were making a lot of noise. Today it's different. Relationships with the city [Granger] can't be any better.[84]

The pages in KDNA's program guides are visual and sonic evidence of an active community. On Saturdays and Sundays, the programming schedule is loud with musical programs such as *Música Variada (Varied Music)* and *Arriba el Telón (Raise the Curtain)* linking listeners back to their homelands as well as other places in Latin America. Latin American–focused programming like *Revista Latina (Latin Review)*, *Selecciones Interamericanas (Inter-American Selections)*, and *Qué Tal America (Hello America)* demonstrate this connection. For instance, local Latino-owned businesses appear throughout the pages of the 1980 program guide. The advertising for La Rosita Bakery reads "La Rosita Bakery: menudo y barbacoa, tamales, Mexican imports, records and tapes, tostadas, tortillas, tacos, enchiladas, Mexican pastry [sic], plus a recreation room, pool tables and music box."[85] These materials breathe life into the archive by reminding us of the intimate, everyday, and perhaps even mundane lives of Chicanas/os in Eastern Washington.

These materials also serve as a record of daily life that was not only about struggle and exploitation, but of cultural pleasures of food, music, dancing, singing, and living. What Radio Cadena reveals is that this audience listened to *rancheras* early on weekday mornings as they toiled the fields and found reprieve from work by dancing to *cumbias* on Saturday and Sunday afternoons. Cultural traditions and celebrations mark the established presence of Mexicano and Chicana/o communities in the Pacific Northwest, including *fiestas Mexicanas*, baptisms and other religious ceremonies, and businesses catering to a new clientele. For people to be able to tune the dial in to broadcasts in their language and hear music, programs, and radio personalities sound out their language and culture meant that indeed a budding Chicana/o community existed in the Yakima Valley.

KDNA emerged as a political project with direct ties to the migration of Tejana/o farmworkers to the Pacific Northwest. Not only did KDNA exist in a time line of community radio production in the United States, but it also exemplifies a different historiography of radio that attends to the unique aesthetics of Chicana/o community radio programming and listens to community radio's third-world roots. Linguistically and musically, KDNA specialized in Mexican and Chicana/o programming, making it an important space of analysis in studies of Chicana/o cultural production. These cultural practices are important to an understanding of how marginalized farmworkers utilized community radio to navigate discriminatory social structures. Radio was not only a medium that provided entertainment but also a site of active resistance that continues today.

Finally, the images of Radio Cadena being physically built—the radio tower on top of Ahtanum Ridge with the fields in the background—highlight the spatial dimensions of Radio Cadena as a political project. In her incisive theorizing about sound and spatial entitlement in Los Angeles, Gaye Theresa Johnson argues, "Spatial entitlement is a way in which marginalized communities have created new collectivities based not just upon eviction and exclusion from physical places, but also new and imaginative uses of technology, creativity, and spaces."[86] The fields of the Yakima Valley, particularly the crops that demanded manual labor, altered the fabric of the Pacific Northwest in at least two ways: First, it created a channel and a need for cheap labor, and as a result, many Tejana/o, Chicana/o, and later Mexican immigrant communities migrated to the Pacific Northwest. Second, the fields were also ripe for a particular kind of media activism never before seen in this region or in the United States—a full-time Spanish-language educational community radio station that would alter the physical landscape and cultural soundscape of the Yakima Valley with a reverberation of activity and radio programming that reflected the needs and interests of Chicanas/os in the region.

Radio Cadena created a soundscape of the Chicana/o movement in the Yakima Valley through the voices of farmworkers carried over the airwaves across the fields through Spanish-language programming. Ultimately, this constituted a spatial entitlement that created a "critical sonic narrative" of the Chicano movement, which is why, as Johnson notes, radio is central to spatial entitlement in Black and Brown communities.[87] In the Pacific Northwest, spatial entitlement reverberated physically and aurally via KDNA's community radio airwaves that transmitted this community's narratives of struggle, activism, and change. Although farmworkers in the Yakima Valley experienced poverty and marginalization resulting from low wages, poor working conditions, and other structural inequities—including exclusions from physical spaces—through Radio Cadena, they creatively adopted radio technologies and claimed aural spaces that built communities of resistance. As such the station, and particularly its Chicana radio praxis, offers important insights into the media soundscapes of the Chicano movement.

Not only was Rosa Ramón a leader at her own radio station, she also became instrumental within the national Spanish-language community radio station network. Ramón's life experiences as a farmworker, her successful completion of high school, and her community organizing work proved invaluable to her practice of Chicana radio activism as KDNA's first station manager and as the first Chicana to ever hold such a position. As station manager, Ramón selected a team of producers, engineers, and staff who believed in KDNA's goal to create programming and content for the local community that was inclusive of women (*Mujer*) and children (*El Jardín de los Niños*). Because of their lived experience as migrants, the cofounders of Radio Cadena understood that radio was an accessible tool for farmworkers who had little access to other media.

At the same time, they reworked this communication model by fostering dialectical media-making: producers as listeners and listeners as producers. With a growing population of Spanish-speaking communities resulting from an increased need for migrant labor in the region, KDNA used its Spanish-language radio platform to reflect the sociopolitical and cultural needs of this shifting demographic. The social conditions in the Northwest, including cold temperatures and the lack of a marked cultural and Spanish-speaking community, meant that the Pacific Northwest was very different from the Southwest.[88] This distinction, along with the lack of a commercial Spanish-language radio market like those prominent in the Southwest, provided the conditions for Chicano movement organizers in the Yakima Valley to embark on a journey to create Radio Cadena, which would later be known as *la voz del campesino* (the voice of the farmworker). The Chicano movement, community media activism, and the development of public radio all fused together at KDNA, sounding out a call for social change in the Yakima Valley.

The first radio programs produced by Chicanas and Chicanos targeting newly politicized Mexican American first-generation college students, community activists, and Spanish-speaking communities were broadcast throughout rural farmworker regions across the western United States. Chicano-owned and -operated community radio stations KBBF 89.1 FM in Santa Rosa, California (1973), and KDNA 91.9 FM in Granger, Washington (1979), were launched by activists and community organizers who became radio broadcasters overnight, producing programming to educate, organize, politically awaken, and entertain farmworker communities. Young Chicana broadcasters at both stations created content unique to their lived experiences as bicultural women with radio programs like *Mujer* at KDNA and *Somos Chicanas* (*We Are Chicanas*) at KBBF while developing a Chicana radio praxis that centered them in the production process. This chapter uncovers how radio was used during the Chicano movement, tracing the impact of Chicano community radio and the way that the tactics developed during this time. With this context, the radio production strategies developed at KDNA that elevated women's voices are discussed next in chapter 2. The lasting impact of feminista frequencies practices heard on air today and in current podcasts, along with how these community radio production tactics are reproduced and repurposed by more recent community media activists, is discussed in chapter 3.

CHAPTER 2

BROTANDO DEL SILENCIO (EMERGING FROM SILENCE)

CHICANA RADIO PRAXIS IN COMMUNITY PUBLIC BROADCASTING

> The very first time I did the news live, . . . I was very, very nervous and after my news was over, I came out and Rosa and Estella were waiting for me at the door and they were applauding me, and that made me feel really good because I get a lot of support from them and I think that's what keeps me going.
>
> CELIA PRIETO,
> *Women of Radio KDNA* radio program segment

CHICANAS WHO STEPPED UP TO THE MICROPHONE FOR THE FIRST time were not only hearing their own voices audibly broadcasted over public airwaves, they also were announcing the arrival of a sonically distinct Chicana public sphere. While Mexicanas and Chicanas have made important contributions to commercial radio broadcasting since its inception, radio in the 1970s was transformed with the ushering in of community-based public broadcasting, a format where Chicana producers thrived. For Chicana radio broadcasters like Celia Prieto, entry into community radio production was facilitated by a supportive environment of women learning side by side the basics of radio production and cheering each other on after completing a news segment. As Prieto powerfully acknowledges above, station manager Rosa Ramón's and producer Estella Del Villar's affirming applause "made me feel really good," and their community of Chicana radio producers was a source of support and sustenance. This is one of the processes of Chicana radio praxis: macro- and micro-level interventions in radio broadcasting informed by Chicanas in leadership and production roles at community radio stations.

Working-class women of Mexican descent may not be the first population that comes to mind when the deployment of feminist tactics in community radio is considered. Yet at Radio Cadena, Chicanas altered the cultural soundscape of public broadcasting by creating Chicana-focused radio programs designed to reach farmworker women. The impact of radio programming by, for, and about farmworker women extended beyond entertainment and into the realm of care. KDNA's radio producers cared about their listeners' health, well-being, and livelihoods to the point that listeners would come to the radio station seeking advice on everything from accessing migrant farmworker social services to seeking help finding a lost puppy or even purchasing a hog. Indeed, this form of connected and community-building radio production is the result of a Chicana radio praxis developed by the women of Radio Cadena. As leaders of emergent public radio broadcast stations, their model of community-based production included training women as producers and technical staff, programming for Chicanas and farmworkers—segments of the population that had not been addressed by mass media—and implementing antisexist radio station policies. With Chicanas at the helm at Radio Cadena, media production's long-established borders of race, class, and gender that had prevented women from learning the skills to be a producer, host, or station manager were transgressed. This public broadcasting model centered on Chicana community radio producers who made inroads into highly selective, male-dominated public media structures while revolutionizing community radio programming.

To break into a male-dominated industry, Chicana broadcasters developed strategies of inclusion that, taken together, underscore a Chicana radio praxis. This not only presents a distinct model of activism and leadership, it adds new depth to the history of the Chicano movement and second-wave women's activism by clearly delineating women's involvement in community radio stations. Indeed, Chicana radio praxis stands at the intersection of these movements, audibly shifting our understanding of both. Chicana broadcasters crafted a radio praxis that centered critiques of gender at the intersections of race, ethnicity, class, citizenship, and sexuality. These subjectivities were informed by their experiences as working-class Chicana migrant and Mexicana immigrant farmworker women. By intentionally passing the mic to Chicanas and Mexicanas in the Pacific Northwest, the Chicana radio praxis at KDNA moved them from margin to center and highlighted their unique experiences as migrant and immigrant women of Mexican descent in the Pacific Northwest.

What follows is a new line of inquiry into Chicanas and their tactics to imagine the possibilities of community broadcasting for Chicanas/os living and working in rural areas in the United States. Focusing on Chicana radio producers allows a reimagining of women's activism through the mediated register of community radio production and an intersectional analysis of the women involved in the production process. Interviews with Chicana radio producers, examples of radio programs, and archival research provide rich resources for mining feminist histories within community radio. The experiences of Chicana radio producers at KDNA were gathered from oral history interviews, audio recordings, photographs, and newspaper articles, all of which animate women's active participation in producing community radio. Indeed, women taught each other the technical skills of radio production in order to produce the cutting-edge programming they desired.

Chicana radio producers, station managers, news directors, and volunteers shaped a feminist consciousness at KDNA as they developed their own brand of on-air Chicana feminism. Chicanas at Radio Cadena imagined the radical possibilities of community radio broadcasting by actively including women not only as listeners but also as producers. Chicana radio broadcasters engaged in collective media practices that fostered a community of support for women producers. Women—armed with knowledge of how sexism and racism pervaded their lives—knew they needed collective action to ensure their equal participation in community radio.

Chicana radio praxis emerged as part of 1960s–'70s feminist movements typically referred to as the "second wave," and yet their activism is absent from the record. This silencing is in large part due to the marginal role of community radio within feminist and Chicano movement scholarship. In fact, Chicana radio praxis calls on us to listen to "waves" not as temporally fixed markers of social activism but as sound waves that continue to reverberate across spaces and temporalities as feminista frequencies. The work of Chicana radio producers redefines the boundaries of women's activism by problematizing the waves model and placing Chicanas in community radio broadcasting at the center of analysis. This, in turn, creates new conditions for exploring the relationship between technology and praxis: Why have Chicanas living in rural areas like Eastern Washington been excluded from feminist narratives? What do their narratives tell us about technology and activism?

The women behind Radio Cadena's Chicana feminist radio production processes understood the power and impact of community radio. Working-class women as community radio broadcasters produced programs that sonically conveyed the advocacy work they performed in the community as farmworker organizers, child-welfare advocates, and student activists. Consequently, the radio airwaves became a forum for public advocacy, a characteristic that echoed among other Chicana/o-controlled community and Spanish-language radio stations in the 1970s.[1] Chicana radio producers honed a feminist praxis that changed the soundscape of community radio and that inspired them to change their lived conditions by leaving abusive relationships, seeking new career possibilities outside of low-wage farm labor, and attending institutions of higher education.

Chicana radio producers at KDNA built community with farmworkers in the Yakima Valley and enacted a Chicana radio praxis in four ways. First, at Radio Cadena many Chicanas involved in the early days of Chicana/o community radio were founding members or in leadership positions as station managers, news directors, on-air personalities, and producers. Second, Chicana radio activists trained other women as radio producers, a practice that ensured technical skills would not be limited to specific individuals while also guaranteeing women's continued involvement in the production process. Third, Chicana radio producers—armed with the technical skills to create high-quality radio broadcasts—produced programming specifically for women in their communities. Fourth, along with programming, Chicana radio producers pushed for antisexist policies at the station, starting with banning sexist music from the airwaves. As a technology, radio provided a platform for women to develop a Chicana voice that was public in its reach but, at the same time, could be tuned into the private sphere of the home and even places of employment like the fields, canneries, and packinghouses.

Chicana radio praxis reveals the processes and strategies deployed by Chicanas, making the act of creating community radio important to the understanding of media production in the United States. Here, the lens pivots to community radio, showing Chicanas as early adopters and innovators of community radio platforms. A critical genealogy of Chicana radio producers reveals their instrumentality in excavating a history of community radio activism that was deeply engaged with 1960s–'70s political mobilizations, and it provides an in-depth analysis of the strategies Chicanas used to create spaces for women at the radio station, which had an impact on their lives. Chicana radio praxis involves women creating a network of support and communication through community radio programming— programming that went beyond the walls of the recording studio and radios by activating networks of care, knowledge, and skill sharing.

Women shaped the leadership, training and hiring, programming, and organizational policies at Radio Cadena because they grounded their media praxis in their embodied, lived experiences, which were far more diverse and robust than what is typically attributed to Latinas. The submissive and docile Latina womanhood that continues to be shown in mainstream media was silenced at Radio Cadena. Therefore, the social location (i.e., as working-class women farmworkers) from which Chicana radio producers approached their work at KDNA reveals how radio is a source of cultural forms involved in knowledge production. A concluding discussion and analysis of the sexism and patriarchy in community radio activism ends with the broader implications of learning from and enacting new iterations of Chicana radio praxis to present and future community media productions. The overview below of Chicana radio praxis provides a framework for exploring in detail Chicanas' distinctive engagement with community radio broadcasting. The *Women of Radio KDNA* program is an example of how KDNA's *campesina* radio producers demystified the radio production process as well as appropriated broadcasting technologies to serve the needs of Chicana/o communities in Eastern Washington.

CHICANA RADIO PRAXIS: CHICANAS IN LEADERSHIP AT COMMUNITY RADIO STATIONS

Poised and confident in her blazer and tie, Radio Cadena station manager Rosa Ramón appeared on *Reflexión (Reflection)*, a public access television program produced by ABC channel 35 in Yakima in December 1980, on the eve of the station's one-year anniversary of producing community-based Spanish-language broadcasts. The sole woman on the panel, Ramón is the public face of KDNA, skillfully sharing with Spanish-speaking audiences the station's important work in bringing communication technologies to the Yakima Valley. Another panelist, Professor Juan Pérez, shares with Ramón the joys of turning on the radio, tuning to KDNA, and listening to music and programming free of commercials. Because noncommercial community radio was a newer form of public broadcasting at the time, Ramón explained how this type of station functions and how they were able to attain that classification to air commercial-free programming: "KDNA is licensed to be a station without commercials, or a public station, and there are three reasons why we are a public station: One is because it was easier to get a permit to build a public broadcast station. The second is that KDNA wanted to place their efforts in producing programs that the community deserves, such as education programs, cultural programs, and information programs. And the third is that we want KDNA to continue to have radio communications training programs for our people."[2] This televised moment marks a significant shift in radio broadcasting. First, FM community radio broadcasting offered educational public radio, an alternative to profit-driven commercial radio on the FM and AM dials. Second, a Chicana—perhaps the *first* Chicana radio station manager in the United States—was the public face and voice of a community radio station licensed to and created for, by, and about Chicanas and Chicanos. The training program, in particular, opened the radio station's doors for Chicanas interested in careers in radio broadcasting.

Rosa Ramón's lived experience offers an important point of entry in uncovering a genealogy of Chicana radio broadcasters. Her insights into KDNA's efforts to make women central in programming and staffing point to the interventions she created within a community radio structure that was largely male-dominated. Because Ramón was aware of the gender inequity pervasive in radio, and in her community more broadly, she made a conscious effort to recruit women into positions of leadership and production. This gender consciousness is tied to her lived experiences as a child migrant farmworker who harvested labor-intensive crops in the Yakima Valley like asparagus alongside her parents and siblings. Ramón also recruited her family's assistance at Radio Cadena, especially her sisters Amelia Ramón and Cecilia Ramón.

A sound recording produced by Chicanas at Radio Cadena for a women's conference in approximately 1984, referred to here as the *Women of Radio KDNA* program, provides much sonic evidence of women's experiences in community broadcasting. The program follows a day-in-the-life structure whereby audiences are introduced to KDNA's daily operations through interviews with women station employees. Station manager Rosa Ramón hosts the program, and her narration acts as a sonic walk-through of the station, introducing listeners to the work and lives of María Estela Rebollosa (producer and on-air personality), Celia Prieto (public affairs producer), and Estella Del Villar (producer and music director). The program sonically produces a distinct understanding of public broadcasting by centering the experiences of women community radio producers. It includes a breakdown of the radio production process as well as sound clips from KDNA radio programs produced by these broadcasters. The ten-minute segment ends with a call to other Chicanas to claim their voices by imagining themselves as radio producers working in communications, which Estella Del Villar notes "is a way of *brotando del silencio* (emerging from silence)."[3] The fluidity of language and the seamless transition between English and Spanish imagines a bilingual audience that does not need translation. The women at KDNA offered insights into what it meant for Chicanas and Mexicanas to have access to the airwaves, while the audience learns about the actual labor in their detailed account of the radio production process.

Inspired by Chicana radio broadcasters' collective process of producing community radio, I listened to the *Women of Radio KDNA* program various times alone and with a listening group I formed with my colleagues.[4] I gained access to this "sonic treasure" when Rosa Ramón digitized this radio segment from her personal archives.[5] Upon opening the email that contained the sonic evidence we had searched for, I quickly downloaded the file and pressed play on my computer. The voices emerging through the digital speakers solidified my analysis of women's community radio labor as Chicana radio praxis. As a radio producer myself, listening to the voices of Rosa Ramón, María Estela Rebollosa, Celia Prieto, and Estella Del Villar from over thirty years ago was a reminder of the power of sound to transport listeners to a historical moment when Chicanas were carving spaces for themselves within public broadcasting.[6] For the listener who is not the typically imagined media producer—working-class women, migrants, and immigrants—there is power in hearing what exactly goes into making a radio program. By demystifying the production process, the program invites the listener to imagine herself as a radio producer. The program is a "how-to" of the production process that provides the tools to produce radio by laying out the steps involved in making a radio program: from writing and recording to editing the final radio version. This collaborative feminist praxis is integral to Chicana radio praxis, which promotes an inclusive ethos of radio making: "If I can produce radio, so can you." Ramón's leadership was instrumental in including women in the production process in addition to centering their concerns across all of KDNA's programming.

As a community radio station for Spanish-speaking farmworkers in the Yakima Valley, Radio Cadena had an active intention to include women in all aspects of the station's establishment and production. Ramón notes, "Right from the very beginning, we wanted to make sure that women had just as much an open door as men."[7] As station manager, Ramón was the public face for the radio station, a role heard in the *Women of Radio KDNA* program. In the program's introduction, Ramón warmly guides listeners through the station, saying, "First of all, I would like to welcome all of you to the studios of Radio Cadena located in Granger, Washington. Radio Cadena broadcasts eighteen hours a day, seven days a week, programming the station with educational, informational, and cultural programs. Come in and meet part of the crew that makes it all possible." Ramón's position as a leader within the station is evident.

Ramón welcomes listeners in a clear and inviting tone that also asserts her as the leader and public face of the station. However, Ramón did experience resistance because of her status as a woman station manager. People who came into the station looking for the person in charge were often surprised, she says, because "they did expect a man to be in charge of a radio station because that was really the norm all those decades ago." She continues, "I think I may have been the first, certainly one of the few Latina station managers in the country, and I know that because I made a presentation to a group of station managers at a national conference, and there was not a single woman in the audience. I was the only woman in the meeting. So, yes, women were rare in those days as station managers and in the radio industry in general."[8] Not only was Ramón a leader at her own radio station, she also became a national leader within the community radio station networks.

The women at Radio Cadena belong to a larger network of Chicana leaders in the Chicano movement, documented in Chicana feminist scholarship by Maylei Blackwell on Las Hijas de Cuauhtémoc (the Daughters of Cuauhtémoc); Dionne Espinoza's work focusing on the Chicana Brown Berets and La Raza Unida Party; Dolores Delgado Bernal's oral histories with Chicana leaders of the East LA Blowouts; and, most recently, Rosie C. Bermúdez, who works with Alicia Escalante and the Chicana Welfare Rights Organization.[9] Ramón's role as the station manager at a Chicana/o-controlled community radio station marks yet another node within the network of Chicana movement organizing. Recording feminist activism within community radio stations is of particular importance to Chicano movement historiography because it uncovers new evidence of Chicana grassroots leadership. Chicana radio praxis enacts a politically informed, sonic cultural production within the broadcast platforms that Chicana radio producers helped create. Throughout the 1970s, female radio producers at KDNA brought their community to the airwaves while also elaborating a more personal politicized identity—Chicana—to sound out their experiences of living on the borderlands. An emergent Chicana feminist consciousness strongly resonated with women of Mexican descent "who viewed the struggle against sexism within the Chicano movement and the struggle against racism in the larger society as central ideological components of their feminist thought."[10] Claiming a Chicana identity in the 1970s was a conscious and strategic act, and Chicana radio producers entered new broadcasting arenas with one foot in the recording studio and the other in sociopolitical movements. Audiences heard this dual identity in the invocation of "Chicana" and "Chicano." Chicana cultural theorist Angie Chabram argues, "For Chicana liberation to be written, Chicanas had to avail themselves not only of different semantic markers, from which to imagine new subjectivities and intersected social relations, but also of new forms and strategies of representation."[11] Community radio production did just that for Chicana radio broadcasters at KDNA.

Chicanas' leadership in community radio production not only represents another tactic of Chicano movement organizing, it also enacts an intersectional and multipronged organizing style that Chicana feminist scholar Chela Sandoval describes as differential consciousness.[12] Similar to how Latina feminist media scholar Jillian M. Báez effectively applies Sandoval's theoretical framework to the study of Latinas and media, I extend this application to how Chicana radio broadcasters used radio production as a platform to speak back to dominant media representations.[13] Báez continues: " 'Talking back' becomes a significant act of inserting oneself as a subject within dominant and alternative discourses. For Latina audiences, 'talking back' to media is one important way that they engage as active audiences and perform citizenship."[14] Rosa Ramón's own "talking back" to dominant media structures is evidenced in her leadership styles highlighted in the bilingual article that appeared in *La Voz*, where she has the insight to document Chicana radio praxis across various media like radio and print. Ramón and coauthor Julio César Guerrero, another KDNA cofounder, spotlight the early work of Chicanas in community radio. Rather than focusing exclusively on the women at KDNA, this article documents the important emergent role of Chicanas in public radio. Published in 1984, it begins with a powerful claim: "The Chicano public radio industry is a relatively new trend, and Chicanas have played a significant role in its development."[15] This article is commanding in its naming of Chicanas at the helm of Chicano-controlled community radio stations and unabashedly asserts Ramón's place as the first Chicana to hold the position of station manager. Uncovering women leaders within Chicana/o community radio disrupts historiographic narratives of Chicanas not being leaders or coming to feminism after the movement. Frances Valdez, a cofounder of KRZA community radio in Alamosa, Colorado, discusses this differential consciousness in radio in her description of Chicano movement activism quoted in the "Mujeres in Public Radio" article cowritten by Ramón:

Many have referred to the 70s as the Chicano renaissance period "Los años del renacimiento Chicano." This period provided expression to Chicano concerns in a variety of fields such as the arts, literature, politics, labor, economics, education, government and so on. In these years Frances and María, then college students, became involved in radio communications as a result of increasing Chicano activism occurring all over the country. "In the mid-70s," recalls Frances, "students at Adams State College in Alamosa, Colorado, were fighting for bilingual education, Chicano Studies programs, representation of Chicanos at the faculty level, supporting the farmworkers in the lettuce strike movement in the San Luis Valley and the National UFW movement. It was then that *we viewed radio as a way of informing the community about all these issues in an effort to organize ourselves better*" [emphasis added].[16]

Frances Valdez's insights on the connection between different sectors of Chicano movement activity illustrates how radio was a tool to bring different factions of the movement in conversation with one another, but radio sonically unites these movements in the context of education, labor, and politics. Radio served a dual purpose to both communicate and organize. Chicana radio producers were realizing the decolonial potential of radio technologies that disrupt a singular method of transmitting information and knowledge by using radio to be better organizers.

The gender politics at KDNA echoed what Dionne Espinoza illustrates in her study of the Texas La Raza Unida Party (LRUP): "The fact that strong women were at the forefront early on influenced other women also to challenge the traditional gender division of labor."[17] In the way that Espinoza claims LRUP as a distinct Chicano movement organization where women were able to attain formal leadership roles, KDNA also became a space where women stepped up as leaders and established a Chicana feminist radio production practice throughout the Yakima Valley.[18] Chicanas such as station manager Ramón, producer Estella Del Villar, and news director Bernice Zuniga not only held positions of power at KDNA but they also produced the weekly *Mujer (Woman)* program, whose goal was to provide farmworker women with news stories, music, and other informative pieces addressing their distinct subjectivities.[19]

Chicana radio praxis that reverberated throughout the programming and day-to-day activity of KDNA represents a vital technological component of the Chicano movement era. Chicana producers and their audience demonstrate the transformative power of community radio production and the role of women in a movement that often downplays their contributions. The presence of Chicana leaders within community radio stations with skills to produce content meant that they could implement antisexist policies, such as banning sexist music and ensuring that women were also hired as personnel. At Radio Cadena, Chicana leaders influenced station policies and hiring practices from the beginning. As station manager, Rosa Ramón was able to make hiring decisions that employed women in positions other than secretarial or clerical staff, which women overwhelmingly occupied at other public broadcasting stations across the country, including television and radio.[20]

CHICANA RADIO PRAXIS: HIRING AND TRAINING WOMEN IN RADIO PRODUCTION

> *Yo vine hacerme voluntaria de Radio Cadena porque todo el tiempo desde chica tenía la ambición de hacer esta clase de trabajo. Pide la oportunidad y la agarré. Es una de las cosas que estaba dentro de mí todo el tiempo. Quise probarme a mí misma a ver si lo podía hacer y lo hice.*

> (I became a volunteer at Radio Cadena because ever since I was a young girl, I always had the ambition of doing this kind of work. I asked for the opportunity and got it. It's something that was inside me all the time. I wanted to prove to myself that I could do it and I did it.)

> MARÍA ESTELA REBOLLOSA,
> KDNA on-air personality and producer

María Estela Rebollosa, a forty-six-year-old mother of six, started volunteering at Radio Cadena in the early 1980s, shortly after the station's "plea for community volunteers to maintain programming."[21] In the *Women of Radio KDNA* program, Rosa Ramón is deliberate in providing details of all the women's work: "Now as a producer and on-air personality, María Estela's work includes a character on a children's program, translation of public service announcements, typing—a skill she had never experienced before—daily fifteen-minute production of a community calendar of events, and a daily two-hour Monday-through-Friday live on-air musical and informational program."[22] "Soundwork" is a term that radio scholars Michele Hilmes and Kate Lacey use "to designate media forms that are primarily aural, employing the three basic elements of sonic expression—

music, speech, and noise—to contribute to a lively economy of sound-based texts, practices, and institutions ranging from radio to recorded sound to the soundtracks that accompany visual media."[23] Performed by a woman like Rebollosa, this labor or "soundwork" of producing programming at Radio Cadena changes our understanding of the job of a radio producer. Rebollosa, who loved music and being a disc jockey at KDNA, was very organized and a good representative for the station. Her employment bucked the trends seen in public broadcasting just a few years earlier.

In 1975 the Corporation for Public Broadcasting commissioned a study that assessed the employment and representation of women in public broadcasting, with three objectives: (1) to examine the extent to which women were employed at all levels in public broadcasting, including production and policy-making positions; (2) to examine the visibility and image of women in all programming and the coverage of women's issues; and (3) to make recommendations to the CPB board of directors that would increase the number of women involved in public broadcasting. This study revealed the lack of women employed in public broadcasting television and radio stations. It indicated that women, though involved in public broadcasting, had not achieved the same occupational success as men in the industry. Particularly accountable for the discrepancy between men and women seemed to be the pattern of job segregation. "According to the fiscal year 1974 employment statistics reported by licenses [all broadcasting stations are licensed by the Federal Communications Commission] to CPB and supplied to the Task Force, women held slightly fewer than thirty percent of all jobs in public broadcasting. Most women employed in public broadcasting industries are found in low-level secretarial or clerical positions."[24] Women, regardless of education and length of service in the industry, were disproportionately employed in these low-status positions while men occupied engineering and midlevel and high level managerial jobs. Men were also seen and heard on the air with greater frequency than women.

Although the statistics in this report predate KDNA's founding, they are indicative of the status of the field of public broadcasting in the 1970s, especially the potential challenges women faced in technical positions. Chicana radio broadcasters found ways to subvert these typical gendered practices in the day-to-day activities involved with running a community-based radio station by occupying roles usually gendered as male, such as producers, news directors, and station managers. Chicana soundworkers María Estela Rebollosa and Celia Prieto participated in NRO's job training program in radio broadcasting, which demonstrates the success of the training program in hiring and training farmworkers. Rebollosa and Prieto, working-class women of Mexican descent with no prior technical training, now had access to the public airwaves and produced programming for KDNA. The radio training program provided Chicanas with an alternative to working in the fields.

As a young girl, Rebollosa dreamed of being on the radio: "*Pues después de muchos años estar yo de ama de casa como se dice, pensé que después de 20 años de ser madre de mi hogar y que nunca había trabajado, pensé aplicar para este programa a ver si podía yo trabajar especialmente después de tantos años de no ver trabajado. Siempre había el miedo de que mi edad mía estaba contra de mí. Tengo la edad de cuarenta y seis años. Iba a empezar trabajando con personas mucho mas menores que yo.*"[25] ("Well, after many years of being a housewife, as they say, I thought that after twenty years of being a mother and a housewife and had never worked, I thought I'd apply for this program to see if I could work, especially after so many years of not having worked. There was always the fear that my age was against me. I'm forty-six years old and I was going to begin working with people much younger than me.") The radio training program prepared Rebollosa for a career in radio broadcasting, which provided her with the opportunity to break free of the domestic-bound gender roles that had kept her at home for so many years.

Being a radio producer and on-air personality challenged gendered expectations of Mexicana and Chicana women at the time and became a source of agency for Rebollosa:

> *Mi esposo todo el tiempo me decía nunca vas a hacer nada, nunca vas a progresar porque pues esa era la actitud de él, pero mis hijos, tres hijas y tres hijos que tengo, ellos tenían diferente actitud. Ellos se sentían orgullosos y me daban el soporte que yo necesitaba. Mi familia todo el tiempo estuvo al lado mío. Él todo el tiempo pensaba que una mujer no debía de trabajar, que debía permanecer siempre en su casa y por eso yo lo hice por muchos años, pero después es que el se fue, bueno entonces la decisión fue mía, de querer hacer algo con mi vida. En la edad mía siempre hay la duda, pero ahora ya no tengo esa duda, lo que tengo es valor.*[26]

(My husband would always say to me, "You will never do anything because you're never going to progress," because that was his attitude. But my children, my three daughters and three sons, had a different attitude. They were proud and gave me the support that I needed. My family was always on my side. My husband always thought that a woman should not work, that she should always stay home, and that's why I did it for many years. But because he left, then the decision was mine to want to do something with my life. At my age, there will always be doubt, but now I don't have any doubt; what I have is courage.)

Rebollosa's case in particular highlights this historical moment of tension between cultural assumptions of a woman's place within the private domestic space, caring for her family, and taking these same concerns onto a public platform like radio. Women like her were not abandoning their familial obligations; they were using radio to help their families. They did not buy into white liberal feminist ideals centered on individual progress, but continued a legacy of Chicana and Mexicana collective activism.

Public affairs producer Celia Prieto emphasizes her process and the skills she learned in the *Women of Radio KDNA* program. Her tasks included writing scripts, recording, producing, and editing—skills someone would list on a résumé. Celia articulates the soundwork of community radio production:

> Being a public affairs producer is exciting. Some of the things I have to do is screen three to four newspapers a day for news relevant to the Chicano community plus information and news releases that come into the station daily. I also cover local news stories, which requires research, interviews, attending meetings, and press conferences. Then I have to write my scripts for the two news programs I produce. The first one airs at twelve noon, which I do live on air. The second, which airs at six, is prerecorded. This involves production, which includes the blending of music, voice, news stories with skillful editing to produce a smooth-sounding news report.[27]

While Prieto's step-by-step explanation of her work appears routine, the fact that we are hearing this information from a twenty-three-year-old mother formerly involved in low-wage farmwork changes its impact and significance. Prieto's pride in the precision of her work comes through when she describes production as "skillful editing to produce a smooth-sounding news report." The volunteer-based production characteristic of community radio stations can lead some to assume that the production will be of lower quality. While the recording equipment was neither new nor state of the art at KDNA, producers spoke of high-quality productions as important to their craft and soundwork.

When the station went on the air in 1979, staff included Rosa Ramón, station manager; Julio César Guerrero, program director; Mario Z. Alvarez, news and public relations director; Estella Del Villar, volunteer and training coordinator; Bernice Zuniga, national news network producer; Elisabeth Ortiz, secretary-bookkeeper; Gabriel Martinez, traffic control; Roberto Alvizo, reporter; and Daniel Roble, project director. While a woman did occupy the secretarial role, as the Task Force report had pointed out, at KDNA women also filled technical roles and positions of leadership, which demonstrates the importance of having women in leadership who then hired other women to fill staff production positions, not just as volunteers or support staff. Radio Cadena served as a site for the negotiation of gender roles and was another example of the ways Chicanas that contested pre-scribed gender roles at home and within Chicano movement activities.

María Estela Rebollosa and Celia Prieto are conscious of the labor they perform, and they also articulate a feminist praxis in which being a mother, daughter, or sister is not separate from being a radio producer. Here Celia articulates an intersectional understanding of her labor at KDNA and her work as a mother:

> Producing news takes a lot of time, plus raising a family, but my family's very understanding. My daughter sometimes is very proud of me; she tells all her friends that her mommy's a disc jockey. My family's very proud of me too because they can't believe that I'm working in a radio station. I thought that I better get into something else besides farmwork and I thought I would give my parents something to be proud of, to be in a radio station and be a mother and raise a family and work at the same time and do something that will help the community. I plan to take some classes for communications.[28]

Children are proud of their Chicana radio activist mothers. Recall Rebollosa's comment: "But my children, my three daughters and three sons, had a different attitude. They were proud and gave me the support that I needed. My family was always on my side." Training women in radio production and hiring them as paid staff created the conditions for women to successfully produce programming by, for, and about the Yakima Valley's Chicanas.

CHICANA RADIO PRAXIS: PROGRAMMING BY, FOR, AND ABOUT CHICANAS

At KDNA, women played an active role as content producers, a marked shift from the radio producer as male that dominated public radio of the 1970s. These Chicana radio activists were then able to create content unique to the experience of a specific demographic—Chicana farmworkers—whose needs and interests reflected their unique positionality. For example, as Rosa Ramón explains, "Celia Prieto was born in Mexico. She is a wife and a mother to a young five-year-old child. A farmworker for most of her young twenty-three years, Celia's experience with Radio Cadena began as a trainee in radio broadcasting. Now she is Radio Cadena's public affairs producer."[29]

Community radio programming archives provide evidence that Chicana radio producers did not focus on single-issue topics but, rather, integrated an intersectional feminist approach. Conversations regarding abortion and women's sexuality were already happening in emergent Chicana feminist spaces such as Chicana studies classes. The inclusion of these topics on community airwaves meant that a wider audience could tune in to this content. Because claiming a Chicana identity was a political choice for these women, it was also a political act to transmit this subjectivity onto the airwaves. In doing so, Chicanas in community radio participated in the creation of a Chicana community and audience, engaging in what radio scholar Susan Douglas refers to as the "I-you mode of address"[30] in woman-centered programming and the building of community with shows like *Mujer*. KDNA and the radio program *Mujer* were instrumental in centering women within the radio production process, thereby creating a Chicana radio production praxis that represents a vital technological component of the Chicano movement era and women's activism.

The-personal-is-political took on aural dimensions and was manifested in the soundwork of radio production. The women-focused program *Mujer* aired twice a week on Wednesday afternoons and Saturday mornings. According to Ramón, "Everything in that program was about women, and it was the first time that anyone had ever heard a program like that, I'm sure. We covered all aspects of a woman's life and focused it on Latinas and in particular farmworker women. We did news stories, interviewed local women, we brought in music about social movements. We played music by Mercedes Sosa and other Latina musicians and artists of the time. We did everything from interviews with directors of community programs to on-air cooking demonstrations."[31] According to Mary Wairimu Gatua and coauthors, radio programming is "a powerful communicative tool where women listen to as well as narrate their own experiences in their own language."[32] Programs like *Mujer* offered women a space to explore the nuances of their identities and experiences, much like my own work with Soul Rebel Radio, which I discuss in chapter 3.

According to San Francisco–based independent producer María Emilia Martin, radio programs like *Somos Chicanas* created the conditions of possibility for Chicanas to discuss topics such as community services, politics, and elections from a woman's point of view. Radio Bilingüe (KSJV, in Fresno, California) and KUBO (in Salinas, California) established policies and attempted to create an environment that welcomed women's participation equal to that of men.[33] Community radio production provides Chicanas and other marginalized groups the space to harness radio technologies and engage in the process of producing traveling sounds that speak back to discriminatory and oppressive practices. Chicana radio production in particular constitutes another node within the network of Chicana feminist activism and creates a "Chicana soundscape" of collective production and listening practices grounded in Chicana lived experiences.[34]

By the end of the 1980s, the cost to air National Public Radio programming became too costly for many smaller stations, since NPR had begun charging significantly more for programming to offset slashes in government funding. The lack of access to these radio shows placed a heavier burden on poorly funded smaller community radio stations that had to compensate by creating more programming in-house and relying on volunteers to create it. However, in spite of cuts to public broadcasting that severely hurt minority radio stations, Chicano community radio stations sought alternative funding mechanisms while continuing to create cutting-edge programming for diverse audiences. Radio Cadena, for instance, partnered with the Novela Health Foundation to produce *Tres Hombres Sin Fronteras* (analyzed in chapter 3), an HIV/AIDS prevention program that aired nationally, as well as other health-focused programming that cemented the vital role they played in the Yakima Valley to improve farmworker health.

Chicana radio praxis engaged and amplified the knowledge production processes exhibited by other Chicana feminists. By rooting Chicana radio praxis in a larger network of Chicana feminist epistemologies, Chicana radio producers at KDNA articulated similar concerns and experiences as Chicanas (and other women of color) across the borderlands. However, this process of creating Chicana feminist programming enacted a Chicana feminist radio praxis that includes but is not limited to programming. Chicana radio praxis is intersectional and brings out the intersectionality of Chicana community radio production. It excavates the strategies of women radio producers who worked in community radio stations, and it reveals important and sometimes unexpected sites of knowledge production. Feminist theory breaks down the intellectual borders that, for too long, have labeled Chicana theorizing and praxis as too personal and subjective. By recognizing that Chicana theorizing and epistemological formations can occur in unconventional spaces like radio stations, recording studios, and radio programs, a feminist approach to media production "allows us to trouble the framework, allows things to fall apart, and at the same time put them back together. It allows us to imagine something entirely different."[35] Taking a Chicana feminist approach to community radio research privileges the stories and experiential knowledge of women who were foundational in the movement to access the airwaves. In this book, I contribute to Chicana feminist theorizing by *listening* for epistemologies in "non-sanctioned sites of theory: in the prefaces of anthologies, in the interstices of autobiographies, and in the cultural artifacts themselves, the cuentos (stories)"—and in community radio stations, including the programming that airs.[36]

In producing radically different content from what was available on commercial and public radio, Chicana radio broadcasters sonically tuned audiences to a different channel and intentionally made space for Mexicana and Chicana voices. These women did not wait for mainstream media to produce content for them; they taught each other the necessary production skills to create content on their own terms. For many years, I searched archives, websites, and personal collections in search of radio programs, the sonic puzzle piece that was often missing from my analysis. In addition to my scholarly interest, as a radio producer and audiophile, I craved the intimacy of listening to the shows myself, to experience the vocal textures, accents, music, and production choices made by Chicana radio broadcasters before me.

In recent years, efforts like the American Archive of Public Broadcasting have digitized radio shows from community radio stations like KDNA, creating online public archives that are critical for the preservation of less well-known and -funded public broadcasting radio and television stations. The original KDNA radio show that for many years I searched for, *Mujer*, is now accessible online; with a simple click on the play button, the theme music transported me to the 1980s and I finally had another layer of evidence in the genealogy of Chicana radio programming. An episode of the radio show *Mujer* originally aired on October 5, 1982, with host Esperanza Graff welcoming audiences:

> Mujer. Mujer *es un programa de información y entrevistas con las que componen mas de la mitad del total de la población: las mujeres. Bienvenidos al programa. Hoy en* Mujer *escucharan a su servidora Esperanza*

Graff entrevistando a María Amelia Garza, mejor conocida como Meli y reconocida como baterista del grupo Los Angeles Mexicanos en su carrera artística.[37]

(*Woman. Woman* is an information and interview program about those who make up more than half of the total population: women. Welcome to the program. Today on *Woman* you will listen to your host Esperanza Graff interviewing María Amelia Garza, better known as Meli and recognized as the drummer of the group Los Angeles Mexicanos in her artistic career.)

The thirteen-minute interview is reminiscent of a friendly conversation between girlfriends that leaves one feeling encouraged and uplifted, especially when embarking on new journeys. Meli shares with Esperanza the joys and challenges of her short but exciting six months as drummer and singer for the musical group. Meli emphasizes the importance of *"seguir adelante"* (keep going) to reach your goals. Digital archiving of programs like *Mujer* is a lifeline to Chicano community radio, especially in the case of audio recordings that are often not preserved or readily available.

CHICANA RADIO PRAXIS: ANTISEXIST STATION POLICIES

The last Chicana radio praxis tactic—antisexist station policies at KDNA— is a culmination of the feminist work by Chicana radio producers. One of KDNA's more overtly feminist practices was to implement policies that prohibited airing sexist music; it was quite rare for Chicano-controlled radio stations to have such an overtly feminist policy. KDNA producers were well aware that music could be a source that replicates patriarchal cultural norms. As Rosa Ramón and Estella Del Villar explain on the *Women of Radio KDNA* program, music constituted a significant portion of the station's programming, and they were cognizant of the impact music could have on their audience and discussed the impact of music on communities:

> ROSA RAMÓN: One of the very important aspects of radio, commercial or public, is music, which composes a high percentage of the broadcast day. Programming of music at a community public radio station takes on a more important meaning than just entertainment. Estella Del Villar, music director, explains.

ESTELLA DEL VILLAR: Music carries messages that influence
thinking. For instance, there's songs that reinforce attitudes
detrimental to the community. [*They play a sample of the song
"Señor Magistrado" by Iván Cruz.*] Listening to the song, you
hear a beautiful melody, but that melody disguises the message
of the song, which is about a man who justifies killing his lover
because he felt betrayed. Part of my responsibilities include listening to records received by the station and sifting out music
that falls in this category. These songs are then marked as unfa-
vorable for airing. In our music format, we use fifteen different
styles of music. Each record is individually classified by style
and color coded before filing in the record library. The station
receives about forty-five records weekly. I also conduct workshops in music and program production.[38]

Estella Del Villar, whose career in radio began February 15, 1978, became
one of the first Chicana radio engineers and producers. Two weeks after
she was hired as a secretary for Radio Cadena, Del Villar stepped from
behind the desk to the front of the microphone when four male radio
announcers were fired and there was no staff to cover airtime.[39] Ramón
begins telling the story, and Del Villar fills in more details:

RAMÓN: Estella Del Villar was introduced to Radio Cadena in
Seattle, where she was hired as a secretary through the CETA
programs. Estella was born in Yakima and raised in Seattle.
She is single and has two years of college.
DEL VILLAR: When I got the job at KDNA, it was as work as a
secretary, and to tell you the truth, I'm not the best secretary
in the world, but I needed a job, and as it turned out two weeks
after I started, due to the lack of staff, I was forced to go on the
air. Although I didn't think so at the time, it was the best thing
that could have ever happened to me.
RAMÓN: Estella is a highly skilled producer and radio technician,
and before we hired an engineer, Estella would sub and get the
equipment going again. She has also participated in the training of many other men and women.[40]

Del Villar would become KDNA's main producer and on-air personality.
Ramón credits Del Villar with keeping the station on air in Radio Cadena's

early days at KRAB FM: "She was a wonderful producer and almost single-handedly, I should say *womanned* not manned, the radio station in Seattle. She produced and played music for twelve hours a day seven days a week."[41] Del Villar learned to produce on the job and created health and social educational dramas or *radionovelas.*

While the antisexist policies in theory called for a zero-tolerance policy of sexism at the station, Radio Cadena was not always free of it or misogyny. For instance, Rosa Ramón's experiences with sexism came from members of the larger community that did not want to see her at the helm of the station. A select group of listeners and community leaders were dismissive of her role as station manager, and a group of Latino men even attempted to get her fired. "It was difficult for some of the men to have a woman who was the boss. In fact, there was an organization of older gentlemen in the city of Granger who wanted to encourage the male staff members to create a petition to fire me because they should not be taking orders from a woman," Rosa laughed as she recounted this story to me. "And you know this was forty years ago, at the time a more conservative, culturally conservative rural community and women were to be married at a younger age and I was not, so. . . ." To clarify, I asked her if it was a group of Latino men. "It was Latino men, oh yeah, it was an organization of men, but it was . . . amusing. You can look back at those things now and you can kind of laugh at them. At the time, sometimes it was painful to deal with things like that."[42] Despite challenges to their authority and leadership, Chicana radio producers continued to successfully run a noncommercial community radio station because they infiltrated the structure at all levels. They cultivated a supportive environment like the one Celia Prieto and María Estela Rebollosa described earlier in this chapter that included women leaders, programmers, and staff.

As a community radio station for Spanish-speaking farmworkers in the Yakima Valley, Radio Cadena had an active intention to include women in all aspects of its establishment and production. However, as if anticipating the sexist or misogynist claims or critiques of their work, the *Women of Radio KDNA* program ends with Ramón reminding audiences that KDNA is not run only by women. "We don't want to leave you with the wrong impression. Radio Cadena also has male employees. So we are also experienced with *Chicano* and Chicana interrelations in the work environment. One thing's really important, and that is, for a radio station to be really successful, it takes cooperation and support from a total staff. *Sí, sí se puede*" ("Yes, yes we can").[43] Radio Cadena engaged both men and women to create an antisexist community radio station environment.

While Chicanas and Mexicanas have rallied and organized around unfair labor practices, reproductive rights, and politics, to name just a few areas of activism, Chicana broadcasters used community radio as a platform for on-air activism and advocacy by providing Spanish-speaking listeners with innovative informational, educational, and cultural programming. With the microphone in their hands, Chicanas did not need to compromise their vision and message when they created and oversaw the creative process from the spark of an idea to what gets on air. They fought hard to create this space, a sonic playground in which to be creative and daring in their productions, with no borders or boundaries on what to air. Chicana radio broadcasters ruptured the airwaves with programs that discussed sex, contraception, sexually transmitted diseases, and bodily autonomy, often creating programs through *rasquache* (do-it-yourself) radio aesthetic.

Radio Cadena founders and volunteers on a pickup truck in front of the transmitter shack overlooking the Yakima Valley, Washington, circa 1979. The antenna sits atop Ahtanum Ridge, on land belonging to the Yakama Nation. From bottom, left to right: Roberto Alvizo, Martha Valadez, Bernice Zuniga, Dan Roble, Ezequiel Ramirez, Bee Gee Ochoa, Rosa Ramón, Mario Z. Alvarez, and Estella Del Villar.

KDNA cofounders Rosa Ramón (left) and Dan Roble (far right) with two unidentified engineers, inside the transmitter shack getting radio equipment ready for the first live broadcast, 1979.

Roberto Alvizo, who started with KDNA as a radio production student and later went on to produce *El Jardín de los Niños (Kindergarten)*, circa 1979.

Producer Estella Del Villar stands proudly in front of the transmitter remote control at the station in Granger, Washington, on KDNA's first day on the air, December 19, 1979. Del Villar first started working for the Radio Cadena project in Seattle as a secretary, but quickly advanced to host and producer when a disc jockey failed to show up for work.

KDNA staff in the studio (left to right): Bernice Zuniga, Celia Prieto, and Rosa Ramón with volunteers Ricardo García and Ninfa Gutiérrez during the first on-air fund-raising drive in 1982. Radio programming decisions were made collectively, often during radio production meetings assessing the needs and wishes of listeners. The program *Mujer* (*Woman*) came from this collective action.

An unidentified volunteer inside the Radio Cadena studio with turntables for playing records, a reel-to-reel tape deck, and a monitor, approximately early 1980s. In the early days, KDNA's equipment was often secondhand, and while the studios were not state of the art, they allowed producers to skillfully create radio shows that were innovative and informative.

Roberto Alvizo, Radio Cadena producer, pages through a script while on the air inside the KDNA station recording studios, 1981. Photograph by Lou Niznik.

Bernice Zuniga takes notes inside the Radio Cadena production studio offices, approximately late 1970s. Zuniga, originally from Berkeley, California, with a background in radio production, arrived in Washington State in search of employment and found a flyer advertising an opportunity to work for a new Spanish-language station in the Yakima Valley. Zuniga, who interviewed with Julio César Guerrero and Dan Roble, was hired as a member of the news team.

Radio Cadena supporter Enrique Cerna inside the studios, in a building also known as the "Academy," in Granger, Washington, early 1980s. Cerna went on to a successful broadcasting career as a producer and host of award-winning current-affairs programs and documentaries reporting on community issues in Washington State.

Ezequiel Ramirez, 1981, who started with Radio Cadena as a radio production student, went on to voice one of KDNA's most beloved on-air personalities, El Viejito (the Old Man) from *El Jardín de los Niños*. Photograph by Lou Niznik.

A live audience of children with El Viejito inside Radio Cadena's studios, approximately early 1980s. Encouraged by programs like *El Jardin de los Niños*, young listeners called in to the station, sent in song requests and dedications, and learned on-air how to make public broadcasting a place of knowledge exchange.

El Viejito and *El Jardin de los Niños* cast members Martha Valadez and Antonio Balderas record a segment of the radio program in the KDNA studio in full costume and makeup, circa 1982. A young Ezequiel Ramirez embodies El Viejito in a gray wig and mustache, along with a cane.

Celia Prieto, farmworker turned radio producer, in the early 1980s, when Radio Cadena, along with Northwest Rural Opportunities, launched a radio production training program for people like Prieto who were interested in broadcasting careers. Photograph by Lou Niznik.

Celia Prieto edits at a reel-to-reel tape deck, 1982. Editing and producing a news segment or radio drama from beginning to end required skill to splice the magnetic tape in the right place; there was no "undo" button back then.

Norma Olguin, another radio production trainee (with TEXAS on her tank top), uses the reel-to-reel machine, circa 1979. Many listeners had roots in the Rio Grande Valley, Texas, often finding themselves in Washington's Yakima Valley as they followed the harvests.

Bernice Zuniga reads a news report on air, approximately early 1980s. Zuniga, an early partici-
pant of the radio production training program, became a KDNA producer and news director.

Mujer host Esperanza
Graff, approximately early
1980s. On radio programs
like *Mujer* (*Woman*), Chicanas were given a plat-
form to discuss issues
related to their experi-
ences, along with resources
for accessing local health
clinics, social services, and
child care.

Women of KDNA during Radio Cadena's first on-air fund drive (left to right): Celia Prieto, Bernice Zuniga, Rosa Ramón, María Estela Rebollosa, and Estella Del Villar, May 23, 1982.

Radio Cadena Program Guide "Ondas en Español de Primavera" ("Springtime Spanish Airwaves"), for March 22 to June 22, 1980. This program guide is exemplary of KDNA's mission to reach farmworkers, especially migrant families like the one shown here with Texas license plates.

Inside page of the program guide: Lunes (Monday) programming schedule; an advertisement for El Ranchito, a Mexican restaurant in Zillah, Washington; and an ad for the radio show *Enfoque Nacional*, NPR's first Spanish-language news show, which aired from 1979 to 1988. Chicana/o public radio stations like KDNA shared and broadcasted content like the thirty-minute weekly *Enfoque Nacional*, which was produced in collaboration with San Diego, California, radio station KPBS. *Enfoque Nacional* leveraged a network of approximately eighty Latino journalists across the United States and Latin America who produced news from a distinct cultural framework, which attracted many Chicana/o community radio stations to air the show.

NRO Graphics Department
NRO Graphics Department
NRO Graphics Department
NRO Graphics Department
NRO Graphics Department
NRO Graphics Department
NRO Graphics Department

Revisa Los "CORRIDOS mas FAMOSOS" en "Musica del Pueblo" Dom. 8 PM

Inspirese... con

Musica y Poesia

Sabados 8 PM

JUEVES

4:00   BUENOS DIAS
5:00   LA POLICIA DEL ESTADO LE ACONSEJA
6:00   LA LEY Y SUS DERECHOS
7:00   LOS ENCABEZADOS DE HOY
7:30   NOTICIAS RADIO CADENA
8:00   OPORTUNIDADES DE TRABAJO
9:00   MATINEE FAMILIAR
10:00   CARAVANA MUSICAL
11:00   NOTICIAS DEL CINE MEXICANO
12:00   ACTUALIDADES DE HOY
1:00   CENSO 80/ENERGÍA Y CONSERVACION
1:30   MUSICA VARIADA
3:30   HAY OTRA VOZ
4:00   COMPLASENCIAS
6:30   NOTICIAS RADIO CADENA
7:00   EL JARDIN DE LOS NINOS
7:30   BUENAS NOCHES
8:45   NOTICIAS INTERNACIONALES
9:00   SERENATA
10:00   SKETCHES OF BLUES & JAZZ
10:30   INDIAN WORLD
11:30   HASTA MAÑANA

Inside pages of the program guide from 1980: Jueves (Thursday's) programming schedule, and radio program ads hand-drawn by the Northwest Rural Opportunities Graphics Department, including one for a music show, *Corridos Famosos (Famous Corridos)*,
with a Pancho Villa look-alike riding a horse, and the inspirational program *Musica y
Poesía (Music and Poetry)*.

Author Monica De La Torre with Bernice Zuniga during their first meeting and interview, May 2019. Photograph by the author.

CHAPTER 3

RADIO RASQUACHE

DIY COMMUNITY RADIO PROGRAMMING AESTHETICS

COMBING THROUGH THE SCANNED PAGES OF THE RADIO PROGRAM guides that Rosa Ramón and I had recently digitized, I was reminded by the hand-drawn lettering and images of Emiliano Zapata, Angela Davis, and César Chávez of the ways that my own radio experience called on these cultural touchstones. Radio collective Soul Rebel Radio has been producing youth-focused programming for KPFK 90.7 FM audiences in Los Angeles since 2005. From 2007 to 2010, I was a member, writer, and producer of Soul Rebel Radio who participated in the creation of many radio programs that included interviews, skits, music, and news. In many of the radio shows produced by Soul Rebel Radio, references to the Chicano movement and the radical civil rights activism of Malcolm X and Che Guevara inspired and informed the programming aesthetics. Soul Rebel Radio did in fact produce an entire show dedicated to the life and legacy of Ernesto "Che" Guevara, for which I produced a segment from the first-person perspective of women central to Che's life, including his mother, romantic partners, and daughter.[1] Although Soul Rebel Radio's engagement with community radio broadcasting happened nearly thirty years after the work of Chicana/o radio producers beginning in the 1970s, which mined the lived experiences of Mexican American farmworker communities, their work is instrumental to understanding how and why community media matters today. In this chapter, a focus on radio production aesthetics and radio show content demonstrating how Chicana radio praxis and feminista frequencies threads together the work of Chicana/o radio broadcasters in the 1970s to my work in community radio in the 2000s to current Latinx podcasting and media production.

Through a discussion of *rasquache* (do-it-yourself and do-it-with-others) radio aesthetics, I connect my own community radio experience to the Chicano community radio practices discussed in the previous chapters. I redefine the success of Chicano community radio stations outside the logics of capitalism that render impact and success by the amount of endowments or how financially lucrative a station is. I hear the impact of Chicano community radio in my own approach to producing radio and in the shared *rasquache* radio aesthetics practiced by radio collectives like Soul Rebel Radio and Latinx podcasters *Locatora Radio* in today's digital media landscape.[2] A *rasquache* radio aesthetic approach to making media centers our lived experiences. Community radio responds to the ideological, cultural, and lived realities of its producers, particularly for Chicana, Chicano, and other marginalized broadcasters who create content to combat a radio industry that almost exclusively makes radio for English-dominant white audiences.

RASQUACHE RADIO AESTHETICS

Rasquache aesthetics and practices have been theorized and discussed by many scholars in cultural productions spanning art, fashion, performance art, and music. Theorized by Chicano art historians Tomás Ybarra-Frausto and Amelia Mesa Baines, *rasquachismo* "becomes for Chicano artists and intellectuals a vehicle for both culture and identity."[3] More recent work on *rasquache* aesthetics is amplified by scholars Stacy I. Macías in fashion as well as Marivel T. Danielson in performance art and immigrants' rights activism.[4] I extend and adapt this work to community radio by bringing the practice of *rasquachismo* into the radio studio.

Chicana/o radio producers, including myself, animated the free-form community public broadcasting format with *rasquache* sensibilities of making do with what's at hand and remixing cultural references and sonic expressions to create something new. Indeed, Chicana and Chicano radio producers are connected across time and space because of *how* we make radio in order to create content that is not profit-driven but, rather, in service to our communities and reflective of our everyday lived experiences, including personal interests, musical tastes, and aesthetic choices. My aesthetic analysis is guided by a spirited lineage of Chicana feminist cultural critique that "looks at the vital role of culture in the formation of social identities on the borderlands"[5] and takes up social identities not as fixed categories but as subjectivities in constant flux and formation. My use of the term "aesthetics" refers to the characteristics of community radio as cultural productions—that is, the elements of sonic expression such as music, vocal speech, and other sound and noise as well as the visual elements in the program guides, photographs, and videos. I utilize Chicana art scholar Laura E. Pérez's conceptualization of Chicana art aesthetics to amplify my definition of aesthetics within Chicano community radio production: "Chicana artists' development of culturally hybrid aesthetics and spiritual idioms," Pérez explains, exist outside of "culturally and historically specific elitist European and Euroamerican values in narrowly defined notions of taste or beauty but, more generally, to the conceptual and formal systems governing the material expression of the activity within societies that we refer to as artmaking."[6] Like Chicana art, Chicana/o community radio creates dynamic, culturally hybrid aesthetics that champion process over a narrowly defined homogenous product. The locally produced programs starting with Chicano community radio invoked influences of Mexican and Chicana/o cultural practices rooted in oral traditions, sounds, and music, making producers and listeners audible to one another through a *rasquache* radio aesthetic that producers crafted. Indeed, as recounted in chapter 1, Radio Cadena's aesthetics were rooted in Mexican working-class cultural traditions such as *corridos, rancheras*, and *radionovelas* (sequential radio dramas) and can be seen and heard in contemporary community media productions.

As community radio producers and activists sought to expand the limits of public broadcasting in the 1970s, their radio productions gave rise to a radical Chicana and Chicano radio aesthetics that inspired cultural innovation in sound. Chicana and Chicano community radio producers created new, experimental, community-based radio programming that combined Chicano *rasquache* sensibilities with an aesthetics of care as a core component of programming, typified by shows concerned with migrants', children's, and women's health and wellness. Although produced in different time periods and through different technologies, the hand-drawn program guides by KDNA and the digital radio show flyers by Soul Rebel Radio show a shared praxis of doing what can be done with what's at hand. Even though the hand drawing reveals the earlier lack of technological resources to produce polished high-tech promotional material, it also indicates a commitment to getting important information out to the public. Radio producers engaged in a practice of making radio that explicitly called for equitable treatment of the Chicano community.

Embedded within *rasquache* radio aesthetics is programming that resulted in an "aesthetics of resistance" that Chicana/o cultural studies scholar

Michelle Habell-Pallán describes within musical cultural productions as a double-edged practice that "transforms the dominant culture's imposition of social codes that attempt to define 'Mexican immigrant' or 'Mexican-American' identity and place in society, as well as subaltern demands to reduce Chicana/o identity to an essentialized fixed form."[7] Habell-Pallán adds, "An aesthetics of resistance disrupts the dominant and subaltern dictates for strict, unyielding definitions of identity, sexuality, and citizenship."[8] Grounded in *rasquache* radio aesthetics, Habell-Pallán's theorizing of Chicano cultural production can be extended from one sonic space (music) to another (radio) to explore how "in fact, both punk and Chicano aesthetics share a similar spirit of making do with what's at hand, with limited resources, of expressing ideas and emotions that aren't necessarily 'marketable' and of cutting and mixing cultural references and sounds to make something new."[9] Community radio producers made do with the resources at hand (like using second-hand equipment) to air cross-cultural and intergenerational music and sounds that created Chicana/o soundscapes throughout the Yakima Valley, creating content that was not necessarily marketable, but very valuable. A shared aesthetics of resistance connects the legacy of Chicana/o community radio to other forms of sonic productions—music, radio, and podcasting—as well as to the larger network of Chicana/o print culture and artistic cultural productions like film, visual art, and theater.

Rasquache radio aesthetics also involve creative ways of positioning listeners aurally—audio positioning—through sonic cues such as background noises, sound effects, and other place-making ambient sounds. Audio position, as theorized by radio scholar Neil Verma, is a useful term "to indicate the place for the listener that is created by coding foregrounds and backgrounds."[10] Through audio design, radio producers can intimately place listeners into a first-person experience that engages listeners' senses in ways that visual media cannot require of viewers. In the programming discussed in this chapter, including *Tres Hombres Sin Fronteras* produced by Radio Cadena and a segment from *The Young Women Show* produced by Soul Rebel Radio, *rasquache* radio aesthetics can be heard across these programs through a shared radio production language.

Many Chicana and Chicano community radio broadcasters stepped into the radio station with a background in community organizing. A social justice–oriented practice converged with radio programming practices to create radio shows that sparked social change. The *rasquache* aesthetics of radio are rooted in community organizing: both Soul Rebel Radio and KDNA fundamentally functioned as grassroots organizing and leveraged the knowledge brought into the radio station by its volunteers and staff. Indeed, "a strong commitment to hands-on technical practice and work with radio hardware," argues Christina Dunbar-Hester about FM activism, often leads to valuing "technical practice as a means to demystify technology and create a political awakening in users."[11] In my oral history interviews as well as in my own practice, community radio broadcasters use discourses that affirm radio broadcasting as a space to enact an alternative vision and sound for radio that included diverse voices that would then lead to more equitable lived conditions for listeners. These aesthetics of resistance appear as both overtly political programming—like those focused on United Farm Worker activism and workers' rights—and programming that is less obvious but just as political: farmworkers' health, women's health, and children's educational development. The radio studio allowed KDNA's producers to take on controversial but life-saving programming.

PROGRAMMING HEALTH AT RADIO CADENA

> *Tres Hombres Sin Fronteras. Una radionovela de amor, aventura y descuido.*
>
> (*Three Men Without Borders.* A radio drama about love, adventure, and carelessness.)
>
> NARRATOR,
Tres Hombres Sin Fronteras

The voice of the male narrator floats over the *corrido*-inspired theme song, welcoming listeners to a radio drama about love, adventure, and carelessness. The program begins with Sergio bidding farewell to his wife, Ana María, and his mother. Both women are concerned about Sergio's safety, and Ana María is particularly saddened by the fact that Sergio will not be present for the birth of their child. Sergio assures Ana María that his mother will care for her, to which his mother replies, "*Nosotras las mujeres siempre nos cuidamos unas a las otras. En este pueblo la mayoría de los hombres se van al norte*"[12] ("As women we always take care of one another. In this town, the majority of the men leave for the North"). In this brief remark, Sergio's mother is recalling past experiences of family separation caused by migration. She invokes a familiar narrative for those families separated due to sociopolitical and economic forces. Sergio's mother is also recalling a cross-border ethics of care that Mexicanas and Chicanas have enacted in the face of family separation, poverty, and violence caused by the political and economic state policies of the US and Mexican governments, such as Mexican and Mexican American repatriation in the 1930s, the Bracero Program, and Operation Wetback.[13] With the first notes, the song—a *corrido* or narrative song—and use of Spanish instantly ruptures AIDS/HIV discourse from one that is white, gay, and male to one that is Spanish, Mexican, and not always queer. *Tres Hombres* producers attempted to tackle a difficult and taboo topic through the comfort and familiarity of Spanish and in the sonic musical spaces of the *corrido*. Through language and song, migrants are reminded that they are connected to and never really leave home.

Produced in 1989, *Tres Hombres Sin Fronteras* was a collaborative production between Radio Cadena and the Novela Health Foundation, a nonprofit organization that brought together health professionals, Latino artists, and educators to produce innovative, creative, and culturally relevant health-education materials. *Tres Hombres* sought to address the rising cases of HIV/AIDS among Latinos with a targeted focus on migrant farmworkers throughout the United States. This project included a Spanish-language *radionovela* and a visual *fotonovela* project, both with national distribution, that began airing in Los Angeles in February 1990, broadcasting throughout the United States and along the US-Mexico border region on noncommercial and commercial radio stations. *Tres Hombres* even played in prisons.

Tres Hombres amplified stories of difference within AIDS/HIV discourses that had been dominated by a gay white male narrative. A 1990 study by Merrill Singer found that most AIDS/HIV prevention materials for Latinos were lacking in cultural sensitivity and were not the appropriate reading level in Spanish. Materials that did exist were often poorly disseminated.[14] Indeed, by making the lived experiences of migrant Mexicans' communities audible, *Tres Hombres* pivoted AIDS discourses from the visual to the sonic while highlighting the intersection of AIDS with other personal and structural miseries such as migration and labor exploitation.

Tres Hombres filled the void of culturally sensitive materials that were of an appropriate reading level in Spanish with its *fotonovela* as well as the void of poorly disseminated available materials with its *radionovela*.[15] The narrator describes the series as a *radionovela* about *"amor, aventura, y descuido."* The subtleties of the word *descuido* cannot be easily translated to English because it has other implied references. For example, when a person *no se cuida* (does not care for themselves), the implication is that they do not practice any method of birth control or engage in safe-sex practices.

An analysis of *Tres Hombres Sin Fronteras* provides an example of how community radio programming could be a site of strategic intervention and political mobilization for Chicana/o and Latina/o listeners in the Yakima Valley and beyond. A critical Chicana feminist listening of *Tres Hombres* demonstrates that sound, as distinguished from print, and community radio programming can be sonic registers of structural and personal miseries and survival experienced by migrant Mexican farmworker communities. Moreover, the program does more than document these miseries—it is also a form of resistance. While the show centers a male narrative of migration and health, with women appearing at the periphery of the story, a Chicana feminist listening of the program renders a more complex understanding of the negotiation of health, gender, and sexuality by Latinos on both sides of the border.

Three vignettes from the *Tres Hombres* series illustrate how community radio programming and sound articulate personal and structural miseries experienced collectively by migrant workers. Moreover, Chicana feminist listening practices also uncover counternarratives of resistance to each of these miseries. *Tres Hombres* does multiple layers of work, as a content analysis of three of the program's core themes—immigration, AIDS/HIV in the Latino community, and gender and sexuality—reveals. These three themes uncover the political work of *Tres Hombres* as a multipronged approach to HIV/AIDS prevention. Notably, this approach to prevention had not been present in other prevention materials for Latino communities. An analysis of the structure of the series as a sequential radio drama (*radionovela*) and of its use of Chicana/o and Mexicana/o cultural touchstones in the use of *corridos* and other musical forms grounds the cultural and political work of the series in the unique platform of community radio programming, which offers new insights into the political work of cultural production for Chicana/o and Latina/o communities across the borderlands.

Tres Hombres Sin Fronteras, a fifteen-episode *radionovela* and *fotonovela* about AIDS and migrant farmworkers, was "found to significantly increase migrant workers' knowledge about AIDS, change their attitudes about unprotected sex, and change some men's condom-using behavior."[16] Furthermore, a study by Bernadette Lalonde, Peter Rabinowitz, Mary Lou Shefsky, and Kathleen Washienko reported that "fotonovelas are read time and again by the same person, have a greater effect, and are shared with a greater number of people than other traditional brochures."[17] KDNA and Novela Health Foundation knew that they had to address HIV/AIDS through various textual platforms, and though the *fotonovela* does provide rich data for analysis, this analysis focuses on the *radionovela*.

While the content of the series is important in order to understand how it conveyed AIDS/HIV prevention to Latino communities, the structure and format of it are just as important in order to understand its significance. *Radionovelas* are a precursor to *telenovelas*, televised serial soap operas popular throughout Mexico and Latin America, as well as among Latinas/os in the United States. *Telenovelas* are characterized by a traditional narrative structure of heteronormative love. Such series hold viewers in suspense through climactic plot twists and romantic triangulations, only to end with a predictable "happily ever after" finale. Scholars have categorized *telenovelas* into the distinct genres of *telenovelas rosa*, in which one-dimensional characters are usually representative of totalizing "good" or "evil," and *telenovelas de ruptura*, which have more complex story lines that incorporate Latin American–inspired social and cultural subject matter.[18] *Tres Hombres* capitalizes on the *telenovela* structure with its narrative characteristics drawing from both *telenovelas rosa* and *telenovelas de ruptura*. The narrative arc of the episodes simultaneously references *telenovela* narrative structures and mirrors the migratory journey. The narrative arc, which is inherent in *telenovelas*, reaches a climactic turning point, holding listeners in suspense and creating listener loyalty to hear the next episode in order to find out what happens next.

Community radio programming, and *Tres Hombres Sin Fronteras* in particular, offered a critical sonic counternarrative of migrant farmworkers' experiences with HIV/AIDS, circumventing institutional barriers that prevented this community from getting the assistance it needed to confront this epidemic. In 1989, Radio Cadena cofounder and station manager Ricardo García learned that the Border Area AIDS Consortium was looking for a community radio station that could produce a series on AIDS/HIV targeting Latinos. The consortium originally sought a community radio station in Los Angeles, but when they could not find one, KDNA stepped in and agreed to produce the series. Radio Cadena producers accessed sonic imaginaries to produce radio programming that reflected the experiences of their audiences and as a method to "understand larger historical scenes."[19]

Following a practice of producing programming relevant to the Mexican migrant farmworker community in the Yakima Valley, Radio Cadena took on the topic of HIV/AIDS for personal reasons as well. The son of one of the area's farmworkers, who voices one of the characters in the *radionovela*, had died from AIDS complications. Another farmworker who was a member of

KDNA's board of directors had also passed away from AIDS in Mexico, isolated from his community. García recalls how this board member's sudden disappearance and, later, the knowledge of this death impacted KDNA producers and their programming:

> We learned that one of our board of directors, a farmworker, had gone back to Mexico. Later we found out from his relatives that he had died of AIDS in Mexico. He died alone without knowing how to deal with this new sexually transmitted disease. Out of compassion for the communities that were being subjected to contracting HIV/AIDS, we applied and received some grants to do that type of education. I would say that throughout the country we were the very first Spanish-language community radio to do that type of education. And from that we attempted to support and understand the gay community and we started to talk about gay issues on the radio. And we started to talk about condoms on the air and it concerned some of our listeners.[20]

While KDNA knew this programming informed communities of this deadly virus and could potentially save lives, audience reception to the program varied: the explicit language upset some listeners. According to García, "They started to call us Radio Condón (Condom Radio) instead of KDNA. But we had to introduce that vocabulary of HIV education, you had to talk about sex, sexually transmitted disease, not only HIV/AIDS, but other sexually transmitted diseases."[21] Press coverage at the time captured the tone of the response and how stations dealt with it: "The reaction among staffers, and my own reaction, is it was done in somewhat poor taste," said Ernesto Portillo, station manager of KQTL AM in Tucson, which aired the program in December 1990.[22] "It's a somewhat taboo subject and it's using raw language." Another station manager, Ken Wolt of KTNQ AM in Los Angeles, was also concerned that the content might be offensive to listeners, so he planned on airing *Tres Hombres* weekday evenings at 9:55 p.m.[23] KDNA producer Estella Del Villar described the resistance from some listeners who did not believe radio was an appropriate place to discuss sexuality: "You don't talk about sex and condoms in the traditional Mexican family, and when you put it on the radio, they are really aghast and angry."[24] Even with community opposition, KDNA went on to air the fifteen-part series not just for Radio Cadena listeners but for Spanish-speaking communities across the United States on both FM and AM noncommercial and commercial radio stations.

This type of programming was produced by a community radio station not only because the free-form format permitted this kind of programming, but also because community radio stations typically are driven by the ethos of creating programming that responds to the needs of the community. Radio was an effective way of transmitting this information because, as Dolores Inés Casillas argues, on-air radio programs provide a form of anonymity: "The public, yet unarchived, nature of Spanish-language radio, together with its anonymity, makes it possible for radio programs to swiftly accommodate fluctuations in immigration law and politics. Often aired live, these dialogues carry elements of an oral tradition long familiar to Mexican and Chicano communities."[25] The narrative themes in *Tres Hombres Sin Fronteras* demonstrate the series' intersectional approach, which included immigration, labor, and family separation, among others.[26]

EPISODE ONE: IMMIGRATION

In the inaugural episode, audiences are introduced to Sergio, Victor, and Marco, migrant workers who leave their town in Mexico for the United States in search of job opportunities. Sergio and Victor, who have migrated to the United States before, are married and leave behind their pregnant wives. First-time border crosser Marco is a young and energetic single man who is looking for romantic adventures on the other side of the border. Marco's youth is conveyed in the tenor and excitement in his voice. His voice transmits a naiveté about the immigrant experience. He is excited and ready to go. In contrast, having made the long and difficult journey back and forth several times, Victor's voice conveys exhaustion and weariness. Sergio's carelessness is conveyed in his assuring Marco that he will show him how to have a good time with the *güeritas* (white girls) on the other side of the border.

Sergio, Victor, and Marco voice the experiences of a predominant demographic of migrant Mexican laborers who traveled to the United States alone or with other men, often leaving families behind in Mexico. In the late 1980s and early 1990s, males comprised approximately 89 percent of migrants, of whom 84 percent were between the ages of fifteen and thirty-four, with the average being approximately twenty-six years old.[27] According to Singer, "In addition, 58.3 percent are single and of those who are married, the majority travel without their wives."[28] Audiences are invited to listen to how the "single life" posed threats to migrant men's health and its impact on their families on both sides of the border.

Throughout the series, we travel with the men as they migrate from one job site to another. The first job is harvesting oranges. In the series, labor is often sonically rendered through background sound effects. The sound of a tractor in the background alerts listeners to the type of work migrants did. Audiences listen to the sonic spaces of labor through sounds of nature when they are outside. Disease is sonically rendered as coughing and the characters describing the poor working conditions in the fields. Radio Cadena sonically extends the migration of Chicanas/os and Mexicanos outside the US Southwest, and by leaving the location ambiguous, listeners are free to imagine their own narrative and location. The ambiguity of place means that it can be any place. This opens up the notion that Chicanas/os can live and work in places besides the Southwest. The fact that the program aired nationally meant that the producers imagined Chicana/o and Mexicano communities beyond the usual locations of Texas and California to colder places like Michigan, Ohio, Illinois, Washington, Oregon, and Idaho.

The goal of *Tres Hombres* was to inform and educate the Spanish-speaking migrant population about HIV/AIDS, whereas mainstream AIDS/HIV discourse centered a white male subject. *Tres Hombres* was intended to demystify assumptions about how the disease was contracted and who was susceptible to the virus, and it advocated for the use of condoms for any sexual activity among all partners. At the same time, the immigration narrative was shifting from the Immigration Reform and Control Act of 1986 to anti-immigrant sentiment with the passing of legislation like California's Proposition 187 in 1994, which prohibited social services to undocumented people. Radio Cadena's production of *Tres Hombres* lies at the intersection of these two historical moments. As such, it serves as a case study in the conjuncture of AIDS/HIV activism and immigration activism within the Latino community. The series became a platform for the negotiation of cultural norms, gender, and sexuality.

As one of the first mediated Spanish-language representations of HIV/AIDS at the height of the epidemic in the 1980s, *Tres Hombres* was developed for Spanish-speaking migrant populations along the US-Mexican border. When *Tres Hombres* was being produced, the AIDS/HIV epidemic was rampant among the Latino community in the United States. By the late 1980s and early 1990s, Latinos were contracting AIDS at disproportionate rates.[29] For instance, by 1988 Latinos accounted for 15 percent of AIDS cases reported to the Centers for Disease Control, although nationally they constituted only about 8 percent of the population.[30] And by 1993, this number rose to approximately 29 percent or almost one-third of all cases reported to the CDC. While these statistics do not account for the number of undocumented immigrants with HIV/AIDS, there is no denying the severity of the epidemic in the Latino community. For Latinos, and undocumented populations specifically, many factors contributed to that increase, including a lack of basic knowledge or awareness of AIDS/HIV, including how the virus is transmitted and how it is prevented. Particularly for migrant and undocumented communities, access to health care and other medical resources posed a challenge. There was also the prevailing discourse and ideology about AIDS being a white gay disease.

SERGIO: HIV/AIDS

Audiences became intimate with the effects of AIDS through Sergio's character, a prototypical macho Mexicano who understands sex as power and exerts that power with men and women alike. If he does not get sex on his terms, he finds it elsewhere—be it with other women, prostitutes, or men. Sergio is the stand-in for the myths surrounding AIDS discourse of the time: that it's a gay disease, that it doesn't affect Mexican or Latino communities, and that using condoms confirms that one is diseased rather than simply protecting oneself from disease. Sergio brings to the fore many issues that migrant male workers face in their journeys to and from Mexico.

Through Sergio's character, *Tres Hombres* takes listeners through the journey of migration, sickness, disease, border crossings, and death. Sergio drinks alcohol, goes to bars, and has sex with men and women, including sex workers. Audiences never learn how he contracted AIDS, which means that he did not necessarily contract the disease through a same-sex encounter. This ambiguity opens up a broader discussion of AIDS/HIV and shatters the myth that AIDS is a white gay disease. The character Sergio also highlights the intersectional challenges of undocumented migrant farmworkers. Sergio is denied entry across the border into the United States not only because of his undocumented legal status, but also because he has contracted AIDS. His son is also diseased. Sergio is told, "Go back to your country and ask them to help you." He sees a *curandero*. The resistance in the immigration narrative is the representation of male social relations and how they care for one another throughout the migrant journey. While AIDS frames and propels the *radionovela*'s narrative, the narrative is not constrained by AIDS. *Tres Hombres* was not just about the AIDS epidemic in the Latino community—it also sonically constructed the migratory journey of undocumented farmworkers from Mexico to the United States and back. The episodic structure of the series can also be framed as a metaphor for im/migration. That is, migration, particularly for seasonal migrants who work for a certain period of time, can be like episodic events of being in the United States and in one's country of origin.

KARLA AND SYLVIA: GENDER AND SEXUALITY

In advancing the discussion of HIV/AIDS, condom use, and sex among various sexual partners (including same-sex relationships), *Tres Hombres* reveals radio as a platform for an emergent Chicana feminist consciousness. In particular, Karla, a sex worker who does not engage in sexual activity without the use of a condom, and Sergio's partner's sister Sylvia, who refuses to have sex until marriage, emerge as strong feminist characters in the series. Through their characters, listeners hear how gender roles and sexuality are negotiated. These two women characters in the *radionovela* reveal a shift in gender role expectations through behavior that centers their bodily autonomy and agency.

Audiences first meet Karla in episode nine, "Una Mujer Que Se Protege" ("A Woman Who Protects Herself"), when the men attend a dance. Karla approaches the men and asks who wants to go outside with her and have a good time. Sergio is the first to volunteer, but to his surprise she demands that he use a condom before they engage in any sexual activity. Sergio angrily returns to the dance. When Sergio goes to the men to complain about her, they side with Karla and say that she is probably healthy because she insists on using condoms versus someone like Lucy, who didn't require the men to use condoms. Karla displays healthy sexual behavior modeling to listeners of the *radionovela*: how to say no and advocate for oneself. Similarly, the character Sylvia offers a short but powerful statement on standing firm in one's decisions surrounding sex.

Sylvia first appears in episode six of the series: "Sergio y La Otra Mujer" ("Sergio and the Other Woman"). She is the younger sister of Rosa—Sergio's partner in the Unites States with whom he has a daughter. We first meet Sylvia when Sergio, Marco, and Victor arrive at another location in the United States to look for work. While Sylvia could be seen as a minor character with minimal speaking parts, her role is an important one, especially in terms of hearing a woman advocate for herself about the terms of her sexual encounters. Sylvia's choices and actions as understood through her speech can appear at first to be rather conservative and adhering to the stringent gender and sexual roles prescribed to Chicanas or Mexicanas. In one scene, Marco asks her if she can help him make the bed, and the tone of his voice implies a sexual innuendo. Sylvia is not fooled by his request and quickly replies, "*Creo que ustedes dos pueden tender sus propias camas. Ay los miro*

después."[31] ("I think you two can make your own beds. See you later.")
Within Mexican gendered codes of conduct, Sylvia should not have hesi-
tated to make their bed, in spite of the sexual innuendo, especially with
someone she's never met. However, Sylvia says no and leaves the situation.[32]
In "A Long Line of Vendidas," Chicana feminist Cherríe Moraga discusses
her experiences of having to serve her brother, do the things he asked so
as not to upset her mother. She talks about how this behavior is something
her mother also conformed to from a very young age when typically, after
a long and exhausting day of working in the fields, the women would have
to cook and serve the men, and how even after having grown up and moved
out of her mother's home, she still waits on the men: "I do this now out of
respect for my mother and her wishes . . . the only thing that earned my
brother my servitude was his maleness."[33] In Sylvia's refusal to help Marco
"make the bed," she is stopping the chain of serving or waiting on men
simply based on the fact that they are men. When listening to Sylvia's refusal
through a Chicana feminist listening practice, this is a feminist action.

By episode eleven, we learn that Marco and Sylvia have been spending
time together. This is a pivotal scene in Marco and Sylvia's relationship,
because here we learn that Sylvia will not have sex with Marco, or anyone,
until she is married. Sylvia's clear speech conveys a sense of strength and
certainty. She sounds young but not naive. Her voice conveys conviction
and certainty about her decision to abstain from sex until she is married.
By this point in the series, Marco has received education about safe-sex
practices, and this knowledge is indicated by his views about Sylvia know-
ing about condoms and safe sex. He is also progressive in his view of what
women should know and believes it's good that Sylvia knows about condom
use rather than holding to patriarchal views on women engaging in premarital sex or having any knowledge about sex and sex for pleasure. Again,
a Chicana feminist listening practice is useful in this scene.

While Sylvia's choice to have sex only after she is married may appear as
an adherence to patriarchal codes of conduct, Sylvia's reason for not engaging in premarital sex is more complex. Sylvia is making a conscious choice
about not having sex based on witnessing her sister's struggles with Sergio,
what she names as "*puros problemas*" (only problems). A key insight gained
in listening exclusively to Sylvia's speech is the clarity with which she speaks
about her choice not to engage in sex before marriage. Sylvia is practicing
autonomy over her body, something that Chicanas do not always have the
luxury of doing, especially regarding state sanctions over female bodies by
way of sterilization, lack of access to reproductive health care, and general

misinformation about sexual health. Sylvia's autonomy over her body and clear choice as to when and how she will engage in sexual activities is not due to religion or cultural norms but her sister's lived experiences. What could have been read or sounded out as her abiding by normative cultural codes are now reheard as personal advocacy and Chicana feminist positionality. For both Karla and Sylvia to say "these are the conditions under which you can engage with me and my body" is a practice of radical body politics. This *radionovela* is evidence and an example of resistance.

In the production of the *radionovela*, radio programming is a tool of health information and advocacy, an "acoustic ally," as Casillas states.[34] The radio station and its programming are doing the work the state should be doing to care for its workers. The programming is about not just entertainment but also advocacy for vulnerable communities that exist in miserable structural conditions that then feed personal miseries. With a lack of Spanish-language and culturally relevant AIDS/HIV information directed at the Latino community, Radio Cadena and the Novela Health Foundation turned to radio to dispel myths about AIDS and informed listeners that the spread of AIDS could be prevented through condom use. These vignettes also highlight the educational potential of community radio programming and Chicana radio praxis at work. While producing in different time periods and under different conditions, the radio programming at Soul Rebel Radio as well as current Latinx podcasts are reminiscent of this radio work at KDNA.

SOUL REBEL RADIO

On Sunday afternoons from 2007 to 2010, I'd race down the US 101 freeway from Los Angeles's Eastside to KPFK's North Hollywood studios. Windows rolled down, my car radio blasting a mix of Julieta Venegas, Death Cab for Cutie, and Rage Against the Machine, I looked forward to my Sundays holed up in a cool, dark recording booth. The Soul Rebel Radio collective met Sunday afternoons at KPFK for our weekly production meetings, working somewhere along the creation cycle, whether brainstorming the next show or putting the finishing touches on the latest program, getting ready to go on air at 7:00 p.m. the first Friday of every month.

Soul Rebel Radio (SRR) began in 2005. Many of SRR's founding members met while on a trip to Caracas, Venezuela, for the 2005 World Festival of Youth and Students, where young people from all over the world gathered under the theme of "For Peace and Solidarity, We Struggle against Imperialism and War."[35] Once back in Los Angeles, the founding of the SRR collective invited "young people from the Third World Left [to join us where they] can find their voice and tell their stories in a creative and rebellious space on the air."[36] Just like the Chicana and Chicano community radio producers discussed in chapters 1 and 2, SRR's radio production tactics stem from activism rooted in social justice: "SRR employs a number of tactics learned from our previous and continuous work as organizers and activists in and around Los Angeles."[37] Environmental activism, immigrants' rights, labor, the school-to-prison pipeline, and incarceration were all areas of activism that Soul Rebels engage in, while also serving as thematic topics for the radio shows. SRR's collective approach to producing community radio echoes the efforts by Chicano community radio stations in the 1970s and 1980s. The open-door policies at Radio Cadena that invited everyone into the recording booth was the same ethos I encountered during my tenure with SRR. My qualification was *ganas*, a desire to learn and work collectively with a group of young folks with a shared vision: to bring youthful, fun, creative, and informative programming to KPFK's airwaves.

By the time I joined the collective in late 2007, SRR was a well-oiled radio-production machine, and the group had a flow that worked. The process of producing a monthly youth-focused radio program meant that our meetings cycled in the following order: preproduction, which involved brainstorming and conceptual development; content development, which involved writing scripts and skits, conducting interviews, and getting feedback; production, meaning recording and editing; postproduction, when we produced the final version of the program with music and hosting; and, finally, evaluation, meaning collective reflection and feedback after the show aired. Each month boasted a new theme that we explored in-depth through skits, news stories, interviews, music, and commentary. For each monthly show, we collectively voted on two hosts—typically a man and a woman—who would serve as that month's lead producers. Hosts would keep us on track for making production deadlines so we could submit our show in time to make the first-Friday air date. As a staff of unpaid volunteers, with many of us holding down full-time jobs and attending school, our compensation was access to the radio station. While this entire process was new to me, little did I know then that these practices had been deeply embedded in the Chicano community radio production processes discussed in chapters 1 and 2. The collectivity found in community media created a network of professional and personal relationships, communities often crossing multiple movement circles geared toward social justice. SRR hailed from a community of nonprofit employees by day who were musicians, artists, and creatives by night. Our community connections supplied us with interviews, contexts to news stories we produced, bands and music for fund-raisers, and volunteers to staff these events.

We held retreats or longer meetings about once a year in order to plan out the production schedule, predetermine monthly show topics, plan events or workshops, and conduct a general check-in about the collective's mission and vision. These retreats usually happened at someone's house, where we would collectively make food, hang out, and *convivir*, in the sense that Chicana feminist scholar and *artivista* Martha Gonzalez describes: "*Convivencia*, or the deliberate act of being with each other as community, is a social, moral, and musical aesthetic of fandango [a convivial music-sharing experience] practice and a central reason for gathering. . . . My use of *convivencia* as a moral and musical aesthetic in community music practice aims to bring focus on relationships and process rather than sounds, outcomes, or product."[38] SRR's approach to and philosophy of making media resonates with Gonzalez's theorizing about the spirit of *convivencia*, along with a commitment to creating a space that encouraged all participants to pursue their own interests in media production: from script writing, interviewing, and voiceover acting to music selection and production. Some of my best friendships started at those meetings, bonding over shared music and interests, arguing about politics, and making plans to hang out outside our radio work. I had found my people.

Prior to joining the SRR collective, I too had subscribed to the notion that public or community radio was not meant for a bilingual and bicultural Chicana—I didn't fit the profile of the nerdy highbrow white dude NPR listener. As an introvert and someone who struggles with anxiety, I always felt out of place in many creative spaces. In high school, I enrolled in a drama class that turned into a failed experiment, since I hated being on stage, was terrible at improvisation, and simply not good at acting. In retrospect, I would have been better suited in the director's chair or in the writers' room, but back then an awkward young second-generation Mexican American girl could not imagine the possibilities of a creative career. If I couldn't act, that meant I had no place in the creative industry of television and film.

This experience was confirmed by my first attempt at becoming involved with radio. While an undergraduate at the University of California, Davis, I attended a volunteer meeting for our college radio station, KDVS. When

I walked into the KDVS studios, I found myself in an environment I didn't recognize, with people who looked nothing like me. It wasn't until I joined Soul Rebel Radio that I realized I actually could be the one behind the camera, and being behind the microphone gave me the creative wings to fly into the airwaves. Soul Rebel Radio became my everything. I was obsessed with radio production and learning everything I could from people whom I considered really cool, creative, and talented. Hours flew by as I sat in my room editing—cutting and pasting vocals, sound effects, and music to create just the right sound. While editing no longer involved the manual splicing of magnetic tape with a razor—I had access to digital editing software with commands that correct errors with one click—the embodied practice of piecing together the audio layers to create a story that sonically captivates audiences is deeply intimate. Just as Celia Prieto described the joy she experienced during the production process in chapter 2, I too experienced this passion during my own editing sessions when I spent all night configuring just the right sound without noticing time passing. The process of learning radio production proved foundational for my later work in graduate school, as I engaged in research and writing for radio segments I produced for SRR. My production interests in bringing engaging content to the airwaves was threaded together with my work at a nonprofit legal rights organization and recent exposure to Chicana feminist theory while pursuing my master's degree in Chicana and Chicano studies at California State University, Northridge.

By 2008, when I found myself deep in the community radio trenches at KPFK, public broadcasting had already succumbed to the ills of capitalist, profit-driven radio, its effects depleting the station of much-needed financial resources. The Telecommunications Act of 1996 allowed corporations to increase the number of radio stations they could own, thus consolidating radio markets under the control of corporations like Clear Channel.[39] My experience with community broadcasting in the Soul Rebel Radio collective—running on bare-bones budgets and relying heavily on unpaid volunteers—was not unlike those of Rosa Ramón, Bernice Zuniga, Ricardo García, and other Chicana/o community radio producers: making radio with little experience and even fewer financial resources, but coupled with an unwavering commitment to leveraging the possibilities offered by volunteering at public radio stations to produce radio shows for our communities. On a deeply personal level, joining the Soul Rebel Radio collective and learning from an eclectic group of youth media producers stirred a desire to claim my agency and creative capabilities. With every segment I produced on my own, eventually working my way to producing entire radio programs, I gained a newfound confidence. I wholeheartedly believe that my experiences with Soul Rebel Radio and learning to produce media sparked my imagination, opened me up to diversity, and prepared me for the doctoral process.

The space cultivated by Soul Rebel Radio encouraged my independence and confidence in successfully overseeing the completion of a media project. The show's format that changed topics every month allowed me to bounce around interests and select what issues I wanted to highlight that month. I did not recognize this experience at the time or call it anything specific, but this too was my own Chicana radio praxis at work. In addition to learning how to write, record, and fully produce a segment for radio play, I tapped into a sonic creativity that, as Celia Prieto describes in chapter 2, fed my desire to make everyone in the collective proud of my work. Having an entire month to produce our one-hour show meant that we could fully develop a creative idea, and with an extensive network of Soul Rebels, our productions often took us outside the radio station to record. One memorable segment for its *rasquache* radio aesthetics in production was a piece on understanding the water filtration and distribution system in Los Angeles. I wrote the script with the goal of learning more about how water travels in and out of our homes, often without our knowledge of its usage quantities and waste. At the suggestion of the segment producer, Eduardo Arenas, we recorded the skit inside a bathroom shower stall to capture the echo of my voice and I had an eye opening conversation with water. The freedom to be experimental and playful in the recording process is one of the reasons radio was and is so unique.

The theme of programming health and community well-being that began with Radio Cadena's programming targeting farmworker health issues in the 1970s–1980s, with shows like *Tres Hombres Sin Fronteras*, was continued with Soul Rebel Radio's incorporation of skits and entire programs dedicated to health in the 2000s. During my time at SRR, I cowrote a skit with Laura Cambron that discussed a practice of testing the Gardasil vaccine on women applying for US naturalization. Latinas' bodies have been ground zero for state-sanctioned experimentation of birth control and other reproductive testing for decades.[40] In 2008 the US Immigration and Naturalization Service (now Immigration and Customs Enforcement) under President George W. Bush's administration changed the citizenship application process by adding Gardasil, a vaccine against the human papillomavirus (HPV), to the required vaccinations. Widely criticized for its prohibitive cost, yet in line with unethical medical testing on Latinas, the Gardasil vaccination created more prohibitive measures for women seeking to adjust their immigration status. Even more alarming was the fact that the vaccine had not been fully tested, and many women were reporting issues after getting vaccinated, including nausea, vomiting, seizures, and even death.

Given that the show's topic and target audience were young women, we knew that sharing knowledge about this vaccine would be crucial. For this skit, Laura and I accidentally walk into a citizenship swearing-in ceremony, where we attempt to inform a young woman about the medical exams she needed to complete for her citizenship application. Using the audio from a citizenship ceremony we found online, we bring listeners into a convention center in search of a woman who will help spread awareness about the potentially harmful effects of the Gardasil vaccine. This is an excerpt from the skit we produced for the October 2008 show on young women:

> ANNOUNCER: Please stand for the pledge of allegiance.
>
> RESIDENT: I pledge allegiance to the flag of the United States of America, and to the republic for which it . . .
>
> LAURA AND MONICA: Hey, psst! Over here!
>
> RESIDENT: Excuse me! We're in the middle of the pledge of allegiance!?
>
> LAURA: Are you sure you want to do this?
>
> RESIDENT: What do you mean? I've paid my dues; I've been in this country long enough. I deserve to be a citizen.
>
> MONICA: I don't qestion that, but you'll be paying more dues than what they're telling you right now.
>
> RESIDENT: What do you mean?
>
> LAURA: This administration is trying to make it mandatory for women who are becoming citizens to get the Gardasil vaccination.
>
> RESIDENT: Gardasil?
>
> MONICA: Yeah, Gardasil. It's a drug that vaccinates against certain types of HPV, which is said to lead to cervical cancer.
>
> RESIDENT: Well, that's not bad, is it?
>
> LAURA: Well, I don't know. They want you to pay $375 to get it.
>
> RESIDENT: $375? On top of all the other fees we have to pay to get our citizenship?

MONICA: The worst part is that the people who are supposed to
  screen this drug haven't even done all of the required tests to
  make it safe for women to take. In one year alone, they've had
  3,500 major complaints.
RESIDENT: What have their complaints been?
LAURA: They suffered from nausea, vomiting, seizures, paralysis,
  and worst of all death.
RESIDENT: Death?
MONICA: Yeah, there have been eighteen reported deaths directly
  linked to Gardasil.
RESIDENT: How do you spell that?
LAURA AND MONICA: G-A-R-D-A-S-I-L.
RESIDENT: I'm going to look it up. I don't want to pay $375 for
  something that could kill me or make me paralyzed.[41]

Although the message of the Gardasil skit was serious, we wanted to
produce a segment that was engaging and entertaining, just like the *radionovelas* from Chicano community radio. I vividly remember my excitement
in flexing my creative muscle when putting the skit together: from background sound effects of the swearing-in ceremony, I worked to create the
sonic world I had envisioned in my preproduction notes. Through community radio, we were able to advocate for and educate communities that do
not have readily available access to health education. We programmed shows
in the interest and wellness of marginalized communities—and the fact that
women's reproductive health continues to be an important programming
choice for community radio producers speaks to radio's importance. We
placed young women front and center in the production process, content,
and music aired on the show. This was the first time in my tenure on SRR
that I got to watch an entire show conceived and produced by women. Sit-
ting alongside Laura as she cut audio and edited the show inspired my own
abilities to produce an hour-long radio program. Like the Chicanas at Radio
Cadena, we cultivated an experimental space that welcomed women in the
production process.

The power of conversation has been reignited with the emergence of
podcasts and digitally based sonic storytelling. Latinx podcasts account for
a reimagining of this sound-based format in order to center Latinx lives and
stories. The interest in podcasting as a viable and accessible medium for
Latina and queer voices is evidenced by the boom of woman-centered

Latinx podcasts, including *Locatora Radio*, *Supermamas*, *Chicana Mother-work*, and *Radio Menea*, to name a few that are popular. *Locatora Radio*, for instance, centers sexual health, pleasure, and antipatriarchal tactics in podcasts, visual productions, social media campaigns, videos, and community events. From the feminista frequencies of Sylvia and Karla in *Tres Hombres* to SRR's show, and now with podcasts like *Locatora Radio*, Chicana radio praxis continues to be heard.

LISTENING TO FEMINISTA FREQUENCIES IN LATINX PODCASTS

As I settle in for another writing session in my Seattle apartment, I open a new internet window on my desktop and navigate to my favorite online program, *Heartbreak Radio*, on Radio Espacio, a community service online radio station operating out of Espacio 1839 in Boyle Heights, California. Espacio 1839 is a community cultural space and bookstore with a storefront recording studio harkening back to the days of storefront radio stations across Los Angeles.[42] Latinx podcasts and online radio streaming have renewed interest in sonic-based episodic entertainment, and a new generation of Latinx broadcasters has sprouted on the digital airwaves. In places where community radio has struggled with funding and longevity, digital podcasting has surfaced as the accessible new low-cost broadcasting medium for youth and media producers. Contemporary media structures, while more privatized and operating under umbrella media conglomerates like Clear Channel and Univisión, continue to uphold a higher barrier of entry for Latinx cultural producers, especially within television, film, and commercial radio industries. Current statistics show that, nationally, people of color hold just over 7 percent of radio licenses while women hold less than 7 percent of all TV and radio station licenses.[43] Latinos own only 2.7 percent of FM radio outlets.[44] Yet a renewed interest in audio-based episodic entertainment like podcasts and the technological innovations in digital recording and broadcasting bring back the conditions of possibility for radically different media like Chicana/o public broadcasting in the 1970s. What are the sonic connections between past iterations of Chicana/o community radio programming and the current proliferation of Latinx podcasts such as *Latinos Who Lunch*, *Locatora Radio*, *Radio Menea*, and *Tamarindo Podcast*? Rather than these two moments of Latinx sonic production being distinct and temporally separate, they share a community-based media praxis that proves feminista frequencies continue to reverberate in today's digitally defined mediascape.

My efforts in recovering the histories and herstories of Chicana/o community radio broadcasters is motivated by what I see and hear on current Latinx podcasts. The audio-based programming being produced by Latinx podcasters is related to the programming that was heard on Chicano community radio in that both are produced from an impetus to create programming for our communities: Latinxs creating content with their community as listeners in mind. A lack of technical experience is not a barrier for entry into podcasting, which is similar to the conditions faced by Chicana/o radio producers. Connecting the work of Chicana/o community radio producers decades ago to today's community media productions provides learning and growth from the mistakes and challenges of the past. Documenting and sharing these stories preserves Chicana/o contributions to public broadcasting.

Similar to Chicano community radio, new forms of digital audio production and distribution create opportunities for Chicanas and Latinas to grab a microphone and a recording device to produce content. *Locatora Radio: A Radiophonic Novela* is hosted by Mala Muñoz and Diosa Femme, self-described indie Latina innovators producing content that began streaming via online platforms in November 2016.[45] By feminizing and replacing the "u" in *locutor*—Spanish for "radio disc jockey"—with an "a," they pay homage to past radio broadcasters while making space for this feminist and femme radio aesthetic. They record in Boyle Heights, California, at Espacio 1839—where *Heartbreak Radio* also originated, demonstrating that community spaces continue to function as important sites of access to recording and broadcasting technologies. Their logo blends a vintage microphone held by a manicured hand with pink acrylic nails. The hand and mic are surrounded by pink flowers imagined as a slightly opened mouth with voluptuous lips. Their logo stitches together a femme aesthetic that recalls a tough yet tender *chola* vibe complete with acrylic nails, makeup, and clothing. Rooted in working-class aesthetics that blend cultural styles, *cholas* harness fashion like gold or silver jewelry, especially hoop earrings and nameplate necklaces, and exaggerated cat-eye makeup along with clothing as a form of recognition and rebellion. As Stacy I. Macías states, "Latina fashion and self-styling practices are as much transcendent as they are anchored by oppositional formation, shifting popular trends, and transnational politics."[46] Indeed, recalling the *hociconas* (big-mouth) Chicana feminists, as Gloria Anzaldúa theorizes, *las Locatoras* put a femme twist on the *rasquache* radio aesthetics discussed in this chapter.[47]

In a time when working-class Mexicana, Chicana, and Latina femme aesthetics have been mainstreamed and gentrified by the same people who once shunned these very looks as "ghetto," "cheap," and "criminal," *Locatora Radio* cultivates a high-femme *rasquache* radio aesthetic.[48] They conjure very specific looks that get further fleshed out in their strong social media presences that bridge visuals, including highly stylized photo shoots and short video skits building up the season's thematic anchor. In addition to online podcasts, *Locatora Radio* also harnesses the power of visual digital media through the creation of short video previews to the upcoming season of podcasts. In "Loquitas Anonymous," the titular video announcing the theme and launch of season four, Mala and Diosa are decked out in futuristic femme fashion that includes their signature acrylics claws. As their opening remarks in the video remind us, "Revenge, spite, and a recording device. These were the elements chosen to create a secret radio broadcast, but *las loquitas* added another element to this production: a full acrylic set."[49] Their sonic creativity is coupled with a powerful critique of patriarchy and machismo, echoing these same concerns raised by Chicana community radio broadcasters discussed in chapter 2.

Latinx podcasters like *Locatora Radio* are using tactics similar to those leveraged by Chicana radio broadcasters in the 1970s, creating on-air and in-person events for audiences to identify with and encourage a stronger listenership. Latinx podcasts have even created their own network—Podcasterio Network—in order to amplify their work. Because formalized media networks rarely broadcast the work of marginalized creatives, Latinx podcasters leverage social media platforms like Instagram, Twitter, and Facebook in order to create a community of listeners. More recently, *Locatora Radio* has used these platforms to call out mainstream media for not highlighting the work of Chicana, Latina, and other podcasters of color. Tweeting out directly to media outlets like the *New York Times* and *Los Angeles Times*, the *Locatoras* are asking why their work has not garnered any buzz, even though they are now a powerful cultural institution with thousands of listeners and followers.[50] In a tweet posted on May 20, 2020, the *Locatoras* claim, "We are SEASONED indie podcast producers with a dedicated following, have taught podcasting workshops at a dozen LA Public Library branches, with write-ups in @Forbes, @OWNTV, and a series we hosted and created for @crookedmedia. Write about us and hire us to produce podcasts."[51] These public requests to have a seat at the podcasting table call out mainstream media, but Latina indie podcasters like *Locatora Radio* are not waiting to produce exciting new podcasts and digital media.

While debates ask whether podcasts and online streaming can be considered "radio," there is no doubt that podcasts, online streaming, and terrestrial radio do share similar characteristics that convene listeners based on shared interest—whether linguistic, musical, or deeper meanings of ethnicity, race, and sexualities. Unfortunately, current Latinx podcasts broadcast the same concerns by Chicana radio producers as were tackled in radio programs discussed in previous chapters: concerns over reproductive rights, fighting against stereotypes reproduced in mass media, and immigration issues that continue to dehumanize communities. *Locatora Radio* leverages many of the feminista frequencies discussed in this book. Their pictures in front of microphones are reminiscent of the young Chicanas posing in front of microphones and record players in the 1970s. The "femme aesthetics" animated by *Locatora Radio* are yet another dimension of feminista frequencies in the twenty-first century. As corporate media consolidation continues, community-based productions heard over the public radio airwaves, as well as podcasts, remain spaces of feminista frequencies and sonic innovation.

In September 2020, Mala Muñoz and Diosa Femme were finally featured in the *Los Angeles Times*, with "A Latina Void in Podcasting? The Women of 'Locatora Radio' Are All Over That" highlighting their DIY indie podcast as a sonic space where they "inform their shows with an elevated discourse while making subjects accessible for their predominantly Latinx listeners."[52] Again, themes of gender and sexuality are transferred to the digital airwaves with Mala and Diosa anchoring their discussions of self-defense and self-pleasure through conversational and accessible language sprinkled with Latinx femme speech. They are currently raising $100,000 to launch Locatora Productions: turning to community for financial support is another way listener sponsorship remains central to the development of media by Chicanas and Latinas—and alternative productions more broadly.

EPILOGUE

CHANNELING CHICANA RADIO PRAXIS TODAY

MY ARCHIVAL WORK WITH ROSA RAMÓN AND THE IMPORTANCE of continuing to document and preserve the work of Chicana/o community radio broadcasters is another way of channeling Chicana radio praxis in the current moment. The Chicana radio praxis developed and deployed by earlier generations of Chicana/o community radio broadcasters merits being documented, understood, and saved not only to preserve these stories but to learn from and use them as foundational knowledge for contemporary media practices. The absence of recorded history compels the rich storytelling in our communities, which was translated into radio programs at KDNA that were grounded in Chicana/o community building while highlighting the cultural contributions of Mexican Americans in the Yakima Valley.

Working to preserve Chicano community radio and elevate the voices and experiences of Chicanas within those structures has necessitated a new way of archiving. The photographs and artifacts allow me to create a remix in order to imagine the sound of Chicano community radio in the early days. Currently, there is no institutional archive that preserves the rich legacies of Chicana/o community radio in particular or Spanish-language radio in general. The sense of urgency to find, scan, and digitally store and preserve artifacts I have come across in my research continues to be a methodological challenge. I am doing the memory work in my intimate relationship with the archive and creating an archive in relation to one of Radio Cadena's cofounders, my interlocutor Rosa Ramón. Together, we are building an online archive with the materials we have collected and digitized; eventually, the archive will be located at www.feministafrequencies.com. As part of my public scholarship and commitment to the preservation of this history, we have digitized and archived many of the rare documents from

KDNA's history. Engaging with *archivista* praxis from a Chicana feminist grounding activates archiving practice from being an act that is only about preservation to one that exists in opposition to many state-controlled and institutionalized archives that primarily cement a hegemonic historical narrative.

Research trips to Yakima with Rosa Ramón included meals with her family and former KDNA staff and volunteers. Many of these moments felt like being with my *tias* and *primas* (aunts and cousins) and satisfied my desire for familial connections and intimate moments that I had longed for while in graduate school. On one memorable trip, our search for archival materials led us to Ricardo García's personal home archive: a portioned-off segment of the garage behind his Wapato home in the Yakima Valley. I found myself in García's garage amid filing cabinets, living room furniture–turned–storage units, and boxes labeled "do not throw away, please!" The contents under the lids revealed withered and yellowing newspapers, pamphlets, and reports ranging from Radio Cadena memorabilia to Chicano movement and farmworker activism ephemera in the Pacific Northwest. My eyes darted back and forth around the room as I attempted to take in every picture, plaque, award, and newspaper clipping covering the walls. A personalized mural to Ricardo by Pacific Northwest muralist Daniel De Siga took up almost the entire left wall in the cramped quarters. Mesmerized by all the rich visuals, I was transported to my first interview with García. In particular, the large portraits of César Chávez and Cantinflas displayed side by side above the desk were visual indicators of Garcia's personality and life's work.[1] As we wrapped up our oral history interview inside Radio Cadena's studios, I asked García what kept him going and energized to continue advocating for social justice. With a serious look and tone, he answered, "Wheaties."[2] At first I didn't get the joke—I was trying hard to maintain my professional interviewer persona—but in the corner of my eye I caught Rosa shaking her head and smiling, trying to contain her laughter, since she obviously got the joke before I did.

My search for artifacts from KDNA is an interesting investigative journey of building rapport and relationships with former radio producers. I have hit walls and dead ends in the bureaucratic and institutional hunt for anything relating to Radio Cadena. However, building relationships with KDNA's founders has afforded me access to stories and materials that I am certain I would not have gotten if I had been interested in only the interview. During my first interview with Rosa, our discussion of sexism was brief but profound. In my naïveté, I expected and was prepared to listen to these stories of sexism and policing around the publicness of women's activism. Admittedly, my conversations with Rosa regarding the sexism she experienced have unfolded as our own relationship has developed. On one of our first research trips to the radio station, I asked Rosa if, during the early days of the station, she had considered herself a feminist or thought the work they were doing was feminist activism. To my surprise, she said no. She would not have used that label back then, given the stigma that word carried, but she did believe that the work Radio Cadena did to help the community, especially women, to access information and resources that could improve their lives could be considered a feminist act. These *pláticas*, or conversations, as theorized by scholar Dolores Delgado Bernal, were critical to my understanding of Chicana radio praxis and feminista frequencies.[3] The work produced by Chicana radio broadcasters and its impact on listeners exist beyond labels that often create their own barriers for engagement. Principles of relationality and reciprocity are foundational to feminist methodologies, and these *pláticas* also provided moments to coconstruct knowledge with research participants. I acknowledge the impact and responsibility of being a feminist researcher, as anthropologist Patricia Zavella acknowledges that "women anthropologists and feminist fieldworkers have long been concerned about relationships with informants, and have grappled with the dilemmas of being insiders, particularly when they have important similarities with the population being studied."[4]

On our drives to the Yakima Valley in search of archives at Radio Cadena, Rosa shared more detailed stories of the difficulties she and other women experienced because of their work at a public radio station. I usually could not take notes or turn on a voice recorder because I was driving. The first time she shared one of these stories, I mentally tried to keep track of the details, the who, when, and why. However, I realized that trying to mentally record these details meant that I wasn't really listening to Rosa's story. As a feminist researcher, I made the decision to not be worried about capturing the details of these narratives and instead chose to be present in the moment and listen. Perhaps one day Rosa, along with other women community radio activists, will decide to document these experiences more permanently.

The archival process benefits greatly from being embedded in community building and relationships.[5] Much of the artifacts referenced throughout this book come from personal collections that have not yet been transferred to institutional archives, which, according to Chicana feminist and digital humanities scholar María Cotera, have often created unnecessary barriers to access to these materials. Digitizing personal collections in situ while recording oral histories for the *Chicana Por Mi Raza* digital repository is one tactic to repair the distrust Chicanas often express when working with academic scholars. This archivista praxis, as Cotera discusses, "largely is a response to a profound sense of betrayal that many of the women we interview feel as a result of their past interaction with scholars who have taken their materials and never returned them, or who have recorded their stories and left them to languish in institutional archives that the community (and the women) do not have access to."[6]

As John Vallier claims, "Partnering with community members in the development of regionally based collections . . . make these collections, along with the archives and libraries that cradle them, more meaningful, relevant, and resilient."[7] Projects working toward identifying, preserving, and digitizing Spanish-language radio programming, including public and commercial broadcasting, continue to provide rich audio and visual archives that cement the work and influence of Chicanas/os in broadcasting. Ramón and I continue our collaboration in public talks and conference presentations about our work to digitize and archive Chicana radio. We have presented at the Radio Preservation Task Force Conference and at the MeXicanos 2070 virtual forum marking KDNA's forty-first anniversary on air.[8]

While some Chicano community radio stations that launched in the 1970s and 1980s went off the air for various reasons—lack of steady financial funding sources is often a dominating factor—KDNA remains on air at the time of this writing. Today's programs reflect the same values that undergirded the production work forty-one years ago: programming for, about, and by local communities. However, the story of a radio station cannot be neatly wrapped up in a singular narrative, and what I have recounted in this book is far from complete.

As I've argued in this book, Chicano community radio stations were spaces for the cultivation of Chicana radio praxis that is heard not only on the broadcasts from this time but also in the more contemporary soundwork by marginalized communities. Like the women at Radio Cadena and other Chicano community radio stations, Chicanas and Latinas creating content today transition between doing community work on the ground and amplifying this work through radio programs and podcasts. The fact that Radio Cadena continues to broadcast out of Granger and can now be heard around the world, with the development of digital technologies that allow anyone to stream KDNA's programming at any time, is a sonic reminder that the work, impact, and legacy of Chicana/o activism on the radio continues today.

This book encourages rethinking how media production historiographies, including who's behind the microphone and soundboard, elides women of color who are rendered invisible or not fully recognized as creative content creators. This book unearths the experiences of Chicana public radio producers whose contributions to community broadcasting are largely silenced in histories of public radio. When we speak of the histories of community radio in the United States, we must recognize that it begins with the subaltern, marginalized communities who are continually denied the privileges of citizenship, but who nevertheless find tactics to subvert, organize, and be heard.

NOTES

INTRODUCTION

1 The remarkable history of Chicana and Chicano broadcasters who were archi-
tects of community radio stations as producers, on-air announcers, station
managers, technical directors, and listeners starts with bilingual radio KBBF
89.1 FM "La Voz del Pueblo" in Santa Rosa, California (1973), followed by
KDNA 91.1 FM "La Voz del Campesino" in Granger, Washington (December 19,
1979); KSJV 91.5 FM "Radio Bilingüe" in Fresno, California (1980); KUFW 90.5
FM "Radio La Campesina Network" in Tulare, California (May 1983); KUVO
91.3 FM "Community Culture Music" in Denver, Colorado (August 29, 1985);
and KRZA 88.7 FM "KRZA Community Radio" in Alamosa, Colorado (October 1985). Radio scholar Dolores Inés Casillas unravels the farmworker roots
of rural community radio at KBBF FM and KDNA in the chapter "Mixed
Signals: Developing Bilingual Chicano Radio, 1960s–1980s" *of Sounds of
Belonging: U.S. Spanish-Language Radio and Public Advocacy*, a work that
is foundational to the research in this book. I build on and extend Casillas's
analysis of Radio Cadena and Chicano public radio by zeroing in on the work
of women and the process of community radio broadcasting in the Yakima
Valley.

2 "40 Years Later: Yakima Herald-Republic Readers Share Their Memories of
Mount St. Helens," *Yakima Herald-Republic*, May 18, 2020, www.yakimaherald
.com/special_projects/mtsainthelens/40-years-later-yakima-herald-republic
-readers-share-their-memories-of-mount-st-helens/article_53bc4253-2edf-
504c-90f8-7ab8ac844fa7.html.

3 Mario Jimenez Sifuentez, *Of Forests and Fields: Mexican Labor in the Pacific
Northwest*, 3.

4 Anne O'Neill and Sharon Walker, "Tomás Villanueva, Founder, United Farm
Workers of Washington State."

5 Michael D. Aguirre, "Excavating the Chicano Movement: Chicana Feminism,
Mobilization, and Leadership at El Centro de La Raza, 1972–1979."

6 *Los Chicanos de Seattle* (*The Chicanos of Seattle*), film directed by Jack Forman,
KOMO-ABC News, Seattle, 1973.

7 KRAB FM facilities from 1972 to 1980 were housed in an old abandoned fire
station at the corner of Harvard Avenue and East Union: 1406 Harvard Avenue, Seattle, Washington. A subsidiary communications authorization (SCA)

signal is a subcarrier frequency on a radio station allowing the station to broadcast additional services as part of its signal. KRAB FM was Seattle's first listener-supported community radio station and the fourth noncommercial station in the United States. For more information, see the KRAB archive, http://krabarchive.com/krab-who-what-why-when-historical-rumblings.html, as well as my interview with KRAB station manager Charles "Chuck" Reinsch, July 18, 2017, Seattle, Washington. It is important to note that KRAB's station manager, Sharon Maeda, was a woman of color. For more on Maeda, see https://depts.washington.edu/civilr/maeda.htm.

8   Ramón Chávez, "Emerging Media: A History and Analysis of Chicano Communication Efforts in Washington State."

9   Jim Lynch, "Spanish-Language Radio Makes Waves," *Spokesman-Review*, February 8, 1995.

10 Lynch, "Spanish-Language Radio Makes Waves."

11 Efforts to create Spanish-language media content prior to KDNA launching included La Raza Habla (The People Speak), a thirty-minute talk show focused on Chicano issues, aired for twelve to fifteen weeks on KIMA TV in Yakima; see Chávez, "Emerging Media."

12 Marisol Berríos-Miranda, Shannon Dudley, and Michelle Habell-Pallán, *American Sabor: Latinos and Latinas in US Popular Music / Latinos y Latinas En La Musica Popular Estadounidense*, 35.

13 "Ondas en Español de Primavera" ("Springtime Spanish Airwaves"), Radio KDNA Program Guide, 1980, courtesy of Rosa Ramón.

14 Creative arts-based practices flourished alongside Chicano movement activism with cultural productions in theater, visual arts, music, and public performance art, offering examples of cultural spaces where Chicanas were leaders, including Yolanda Broyles-González, *El Teatro Campesino: Theater in the Chicano Movement*; Laura Pérez, *Chicana Art: The Politics of Spiritual and Aesthetics Altarities*; Maylei Blackwell, *¡Chicana Power! Contested Histories of Feminism in the Chicano Movement* (print media); and Norma E. Cantú and Olga Nájera-Ramírez, *Chicana Traditions: Continuity and Change* (Chicana feminist expressive culture).

15 In my chapter "Feminista Frequencies: Chicana Radio Activism in the Pacific Northwest, 1975–1990" in *Chicana Movidas*, I use the term "Chicana radio activism" to name the Chicana feminist radio work and production style developed at KDNA. I have since reconceptualized the term with a shift toward praxis in naming the work of merging Chicana theory and activism with radio production.

16 The 1980 Radio KDNA Program Guide "Ondas en Español de Primavera" lists employees, volunteers, and KDNA students who orchestrated the station's daily programming, a list that includes both men and women across categories. The founders include Rosa Ramón, Ricardo García, Julio César Guerrero, and Daniel Robleski, while Chuck Reinsch, the station manager at KRAB FM, is often cited as key in KDNA's establishment by facilitating the use of KRAB's

subsidiary communications authorization (SCA) signal. Indeed, the efforts required to build a radio station no doubt include many other people not named in station documents or recalled in interviews. "Ondas en Español de Primavera," *Radio KDNA Program Guide*, 1980, published quarterly in Granger, Washington, courtesy of Rosa Ramón.

17 Susan Marionneaux, "KDNA Radio's Estella Del Villar Breaks Gender Barriers with a Strong Voice," *Yakima Herald-Republic*, June 22, 2000.

18 Ricardo Romano García, interview by author, April 11, 2014, Granger, Washington.

19 Spanish-language radio scholarship is an area within the broader field of Latinx media studies that continues to expand in exciting ways. Much of the early scholarship on US Spanish-language radio begins with Félix Gutiérrez and Jorge Reina Schement's 1979 monograph *Spanish-Language Radio in the Southwestern United States*. It would take nearly thirty years for the emergence of works by scholars like Mari Castañeda Paredes, "The Transformation of Spanish-Language Radio in the U.S.," and Casillas, *Sounds of Belonging*. For a comprehensive bibliography on Spanish-language radio research, see Casillas, "US Spanish-Language Radio," Oxford Bibliographies, 2018.

20 Chicana studies is an expansive field that crosses interdisciplinary boundaries while bridging various methodologies. A selection of the seminal Chicana feminist scholarship framing this book includes Vicki L. Ruiz, *From Out of the Shadows: Mexican Women in Twentieth-Century America*; Mary Pardo, *Mexican American Women Activists*; Emma Pérez, *The Decolonial Imaginary: Writing Chicanas into History*; Mary Pat Brady, Extinct Lands, Temporal Geographies: *Chicana Literature and the Urgency of Space*; Michelle Habell-Pallán, *Loca Motion: The Travels of Chicana and Latina Popular Culture*; Antonia I. Castañeda, *Three Decades of Engendering History: Selected Works of Antonia I. Castaneda*; Dolores Delgado Bernal, "Grassroots Leadership Reconceptualized: Chicana Oral Histories and the 1968 East Los Angeles School Blowouts"; Blackwell, *¡Chicana Power!;* Dionne Espinoza, María Eugenia Cotera, and Maylei Blackwell, eds., *Chicana Movidas: New Narratives of Activism and Feminism in the Movement Era*; and Martha Gonzalez, *Chican@ Artivistas: Music, Community, and Transborder Tactics in East Los Angeles*.

21 I first met Ramón when I interviewed her for the Women Who Rock Oral History Project in March 2012 (https://content.lib.washington.edu/wwrweb/ and https://womenwhorockcommunity.org/digital-oral-history-project/). We have since collaborated on collecting and digitizing extensive photographs and radio ephemera documenting Radio Cadena's emergence in the Yakima Valley as a critical source of information and community building for Spanish-speaking residents. The Women Who Rock Collective and Digital Oral History Archive brings together scholars, musicians, media-makers, performers, artists, and activists to explore the role of women and popular music in the creation of cultural scenes and social justice movements in the Americas and beyond. This multifaceted endeavor reshapes conventional understandings of music and cultural production by initiating collective methods of research,

teaching, and community and scholarly collaboration. Women Who Rock encompasses several interwoven components: an annual participant-driven community engagement conference and film festival; project-based coursework at the graduate and undergraduate levels; and an oral history archive that ties the various components together: http://content.lib.washington.edu /wwrweb/.

22 Chon A. Noriega, *Shot in America: Television, the State, and the Rise of Chicano Cinema*; Casillas, *Sounds of Belonging*; Randy J. Ontiveros, *In the Spirit of a New People: The Cultural Politics of the Chicano Movement*.

23 Our presentations together include "Radio KDNA 41st Anniversary Panel," hosted virtually by MeXicanos 2070, December 17, 2020, and "Spanish Language and Multilingual Radio," a paper presented at the Radio Preservation Task Force Conference: From Archive to Classroom at the Library of Congress, Washington, DC, November 2–4, 2017.

24 Michelle Habell-Pallán, Sonnet Retman, Angelica Macklin, and Monica De La Torre, "Women Who Rock: Making Scenes, Building Communities: Convivencia and Archivista Praxis for a Digital Era."

25 For more on the role of critical archival studies in radio research, see Amanda Keeler and Josh Shepperd, "Radio Research as Critical Archival Studies: Cross-Sector Collaboration and the Sound Record."

26 In the book chapter "Feminista Frequencies," I discuss Chicano public radio work as activism growing from the Chicano movement in the Pacific Northwest. I use the term "Chicana radio activism" to signal the women-centered radio production tactics emerging at Radio Cadena. For more, see Espinoza, Cotera, and Blackwell, eds., *Chicana Movidas*.

27 Dolores Delgado Bernal, "Disrupting Epistemological Boundaries: Reflections on Feminista Methodological and Pedagogical Interventions."

28 See Gutiérrez and Schement, *Spanish-Language Radio in the Southwestern United States*; Casillas, *Sounds of Belonging*; Mari Castañeda Paredes, "Altering the U.S. Soundscape through Latina/o Community Radio"; Sonia De La Cruz, "Latino Airwaves: Radio Bilingüe and Spanish-Language Public Radio"; Monica De La Torre, " 'Programas Sin Vergüenza (Shameless Programs)': Mapping Chicanas in Community Radio in the 1970s"; Carlos Jimenez, "Antenna Dilemmas: The Rise of an Indigenous-Language Low-Power Radio Station in Southern California."

29 Mary Wairimu Gatua, Tracey Owens Patton, and Michael R. Brown, "Giving Voice to Invisible Women: 'FIRE' as Model of a Successful Women's Community Radio in Africa."

30 For more on the role of activism in radio production, see Christina Dunbar-Hester, *Low Power to the People: Pirates, Protest, and Politics in FM Radio Activism*; Castañeda Paredes, "Altering the U.S. Soundscape"; De La Torre, "'Programas Sin Vergüenza (Shameless Programs)' "; Cruz, "Latino Airwaves." There is also extensive work on radio, activism, and the public sphere in other Black, Indigenous, and people of color (BIPOC) communities; see Catherine R. Squires, "Black Talk Radio: Defining Community Needs and Identity," and

on Native American community radio, see Deondre Smiles, "Listening to Native Radio."

31 Chela Sandoval, *Methodology of the Oppressed*, 53.

32 Latina Feminist Group, *Telling to Live: Latina Feminist Testimonios*, 3.

33 bell hooks, *Talking Back: Thinking Feminist, Thinking Black*, 9.

34 Sonia Robles, *Mexican Waves: Radio Broadcasting along Mexico's Northern Border*, 1930–1950.

35 For more on the history of radio brokers and Spanish-language radio commercial in the United States, see Gutiérrez and Schement, S*panish-Language Radio in the Southwestern United States*; Rosa Linda Fregoso, *The Bronze Screen: Chicana and Chicano Film Culture*; Casillas, *Sounds of Belonging*; and Deborah R. Vargas, *Dissonant Divas in Chicana Music: The Limits of La Onda*.

36 Gutiérrez and Schement, *Spanish-Language Radio in the Southwestern United States*.

37 Gutiérrez and Schement, *Spanish-Language Radio in the Southwestern United States*.

38 Fregoso, *Bronze Screen*.

39 Fregoso, *Bronze Screen*.

40 Vargas, *Dissonant Divas in Chicana Music*, 24.

41 Carlos S. Maldonado and Gilberto García, *The Chicano Experience in the Northwest*.

42 For extensive work on Spanish-language radio, see Casillas, *Sounds of Belonging*; Casillas, "US Spanish-Language Radio"; Casillas, "Sounds of Surveillance: U.S. Spanish-Language Radio Patrols La Migra"; and Castañeda Paredes, "The Transformation of Spanish-Language Radio in the U.S."

43 Susan J. Douglas, *Listening In: Radio and the American Imagination*, 17.

44 Linda Baker, "Hispanic Station Celebrates Fifth," *Yakima Herald-Republic*, December 17, 1984.

45 See Gene Fowler and Bill Crawford, *Border Radio: Quacks, Yodelers, Pitchmen, Psychics, and Other Amazing Broadcasters of the American Airwaves*, and Robles, *Mexican Waves*, on how Mexican advertisers and broadcasters leveraged these powerful radio towers to reach audiences on both sides of the US-Mexico border.

46 Fowler and Crawford, *Border Radio*.

47 Ricardo Romano García, interview by author, April 11, 2014, Granger, Washington.

48 For more on the media activism and legal actions behind media reform, see Noriega, *Shot in America*, and Casillas, *Sounds of Belonging*.

49 Rosa Ramón, interview by author, March 9, 2012, Seattle, Washington.

50 Radio Cadena Fact Sheet, n.d., courtesy of Rosa Ramón.

51 William Barlow, "Rebel Airways: Radio and Revolution in Latin America," 123.

52 In the 1920s–'30s, Latino brokers purchased blocks of airtime for Spanish-language programming at predominantly commercial English-language radio stations. The first successful brokers included Señor Lozano, who began a brokered program in San Antonio in 1928, and Rodolfo Hoyos, who was on the air

in Los Angeles from 1932 to 1974. In 1946 Raul Cortez, a Spanish-language radio broker, became the first Chicano to own and operate the first full-time Spanish-language radio station, KCOR, in San Antonio, Texas. For more on the history of radio brokers and Spanish-language commercial radio in the United States, see Fregoso, *Bronze Screen*, and Casillas, *Sounds of Belonging*.

53 Articles of Incorporation, Northwest Chicano Radio Network (NCRN) and Radio Cadena, April 27, 1976, courtesy of Rosa Ramón.

54 The Public Broadcasting Act of 1967 was instrumental in creating a funding mechanism for community-based media via the Corporation for Public Broadcasting (CPB) as a public subsidy for the development and expansion of educational public broadcasting. For more, see Robert K. Avery, "The Public Broadcasting Act of 1967: Looking Ahead by Looking Back."

55 Francisco J. Lewels, *The Uses of the Media by the Chicano Movement: A Study in Minority Access*; Noriega, *Shot in America*; Casillas, *Sounds of Belonging*.

56 Lewels, *Uses of the Media by the Chicano Movement*, 108.

57 Ontiveros, *In the Spirit of a New People*, 39.

58 Casillas, *Sounds of Belonging*, 16.

59 Casillas, *Sounds of Belonging*, 52–53.

60 Rosa Ramón, interview by author, March 9, 2012, Seattle, Washington.

61 "Ondas en Español de Primavera," *Radio KDNA Program Guide*, 1980, courtesy of Rosa Ramón.

62 María Martin, "Crossing Borders," 158.

63 Ernesto Aguilar, "Ernesto Aguilar: I'm a Testament to Public Media's Transformative Power."

64 Research on Spanish-language radio broadcasting in the United States, along with its transnational connections, includes the foundational 1979 case study by Gutiérrez and Schement; Casillas's innovative *Sounds of Belonging*; Castañeda Paredes, "Altering the U.S. Soundscape through Latina/o Community Radio"; Cruz, "Latino Airwaves"; De La Torre, " 'Programas Sin Vergüenza (Shameless Programs)' "; and Jimenez, "Antenna Dilemmas."

65 Lewels, *Uses of the Media by the Chicano Movement*.

66 For more on the impact of Spanish-language radio in the United States and Mexico, see Casillas, *Sounds of Belonging*; Castañeda Paredes, "The Transformation of Spanish-Language Radio in the U.S."; Cruz, "Latino Airwaves"; and Robles, *Mexican Waves*.

67 Dionne Espinoza, " 'The Partido Belongs to Those Who Will Work for It': Chicana Organizing and Leadership in the Texas Raza Unida Party, 1970–1980."

CHAPTER 1. THE ROOTS OF RADIO CADENA

1 Jerry García and Dora Sánchez Treviño, "A Chicana in Northern Aztlán: An Oral History of Dora Sánchez Treviño."

2 Donald Browne, "Speaking in Our Own Tongue: Linguistic Minority Radio in the United States."

3   Bob Lochte, "U.S. Public Radio: What Is It—and for Whom?"

4   Dolores Inés Casillas, *Sounds of Belonging: U.S. Spanish-Language Radio and Public Advocacy*, 24.

5   Casillas, *Sounds of Belonging*.

6   Curtis Marez, *Farm Worker Futurism: Speculative Technologies of Resistance*, 6.

7   "Ondas en Español de Primavera" ("Springtime Spanish Airwaves"), *Radio KDNA Program Guide*, 1980, courtesy of Rosa Ramón.

8   Erasmo Gamboa, *Mexican Labor and World War II: Braceros in the Pacific Northwest, 1942–1947;* Yolanda Alaniz and Megan Cornish, *Viva la Raza: A History of Chicano Identity and Resistance;* Mario Jimenez Sifuentez, *Of Forests and Fields: Mexican Labor in the Pacific Northwest.*

9   Lyndon B. Johnson, "Remarks upon Signing the Public Broadcasting Act of 1967," November 7, 1967. The American Presidency Project, Gerhard Peters and John T. Woolley, accessed May 4, 2021, www.presidency.ucsb.edu/documents /remarks-upon-signing-the-public-broadcasting-act-1967.

10 For more on the migration and settlement of Chicanos in the Pacific Northwest, see Antonia I. Castañeda, " 'Que Se Pudieran Defender (So You Could Defend Yourselves)': Chicanas, Regional History, and National Discourses"; Josué Quezada Estrada, "Texas Mexican Diaspora to Washington State: Recruitment, Migration, and Community, 1940–1960"; Erasmo Gamboa, "Mexican Migration into Washington State: A History, 1940–1950"; García and Treviño, "A Chicana in Northern Aztlán"; Sifuentez, *Of Forests and Fields*; Carlos S. Maldonado and Gilberto García, *The Chicano Experience in the Northwest*; Richard W. Slatta, "Chicanos in the Pacific Northwest: An Historical Overview of Oregon's Chicanos."

11 Rámon Chávez, "Emerging Media: A History and Analysis of Chicano Communication Efforts in Washington State."

12 Pacific Northwest historian Erasmo Gamboa documents that Mexican migration to Washington state dates back to as early as the 1800s. For more, see Gamboa, "Mexican Migration into Washington State"; Gamboa, "Chicanos in the Pacific Northwest: Expanding the Discourse"; and Gamboa, *Mexican Labor and World War II*.

13 For a more nuanced account of the various periods of Mexican and Chicano migration to the Pacific Northwest, see Maldonado and García, *Chicano Experience in the Northwest*; Jerry García and Gilberto García, eds., *Memory, Community, and Activism: Mexican Migration and Labor in the Pacific Northwest*; and Gamboa, *Mexican Labor and World War II*.

14 Antonia Castañeda, " 'Que Se Pudieran Defender (So You Could Defend Yourselves)' "; Gamboa, "Mexican Migration into Washington State"; Gamboa, *Mexican Labor and World War II*; García and García, eds., *Memory, Community, and Activism*; García and Treviño, "A Chicana in Northern Aztlán"; Alaniz and Cornish, *Viva la Raza*; Theresa Delgadillo, *Latina Lives in Milwaukee*; Sifuentez, *Of Forests and Fields*.

15 Gamboa, *Mexican Labor and World War II*; Sifuentez, *Of Forests and Fields*.

16 García and Treviño, "A Chicana in Northern Aztlán," 17.

17 Gamboa, "Mexican Migration into Washington State."

18 García and Treviño, "A Chicana in Northern Aztlán," 17.

19 For more on the Bracero Program, see Gamboa, *Mexican Labor and World War II*, and Sifuentez, *Of Forests and Fields*.

20 Gamboa, "Mexican Migration into Washington State."

21 Gamboa, "Mexican Migration into Washington State," 127.

22 Ricardo Romano García, interview by author, April 11, 2014, Granger, Washington.

23 Erasmo Gamboa, *Voces Hispanas = Hispanic Voices of Idaho: Excerpts from the Idaho Hispanic Oral History Project.*

24 García and Treviño, "A Chicana in Northern Aztlán"; Antonia Castañeda, "'Que Se Pudieran Defender (So You Could Defend Yourselves)'"; García and García, eds., *Memory, Community, and Activism*; Alaniz and Cornish, *Viva La Raza.*

25 Antonia Castañeda, "'Que Se Pudieran Defender (So You Could Defend Yourselves)'."

26 Antonia Castañeda, "'Que Se Pudieran Defender (So You Could Defend Yourselves)'," 117.

27 Antonia Castañeda, "'Que Se Pudieran Defender (So You Could Defend Yourselves)'."

28 Gamboa, "Mexican Migration into Washington State."

29 Antonia Castañeda, "'Que Se Pudieran Defender (So You Could Defend Yourselves)'," 126.

30 García and Treviño, "A Chicana in Northern Aztlán," 46–47.

31 García and Treviño, "A Chicana in Northern Aztlán."

32 Anne O'Neill and Sharon Walker, "Tomás Villanueva, Founder, United Farm Workers of Washington State."

33 Antonia Castañeda, "'Que Se Pudieran Defender (So You Could Defend Yourselves)'," 120.

34 Richard W. Slatta and Maxine P. Atkinson, "Chicanos in the Pacific Northwest: A Demographic and Socioeconomic Portrait."

35 For a time line on Chicano movement activism in the Pacific Northwest from 1960 to 1985, see Oscar Rosales Castañeda, "Timeline: Movimiento from 1960–1985."

36 Alaniz and Cornish, *Viva La Raza.*

37 Casillas discusses the details of this visit in chapter 2 of *Sounds of Belonging.*

38 Rosa Ramón, interview by author, March 9, 2012, Seattle, Washington.

39 Rosa Ramón, interview by author, March 9, 2012, Seattle Washington.

40 García and Treviño, "A Chicana in Northern Aztlán," 25.

41 García and Treviño, "A Chicana in Northern Aztlán," 46.

42 Ricardo Romano García, interview by author, April 11, 2014, Granger, Washington.

43 Jean Guerrero, "KDNA Founder Plans an Active Retirement," *Yakima Herald-Republic*, June 28, 2009.

44 Alaniz and Cornish, *Viva La Raza*, 296.

45 Ricardo Romano García, interview by author, April 11, 2014, Granger, Washington.

46 Rosa Ramón, interview by author, March 9, 2012, Seattle, Washington.

47 Ricardo Romano García, interview by author, April 11, 2014, Granger, Washington.

48 *Current*, "Carnegie I: Membership, preface of report, 1967," Current: News for People in Public Media, October 16, 1999, https://current.org/1999/10/carnegie-i-1967/.

49 For his history of Public Broadcasting Act taping radio, see Bill Siemering, "Bill Siemering's 'National Public Radio Purposes,' 1970," *Current*, May 17, 2012, accessed February 20, 2021, https://current.org/2012/05/national-public-radio-purposes/.

50 Ralph Engelman, *Public Radio and Television in America: A Political History*.

51 The Pacifica Foundation, founded in 1946 by Lewis Hill, is a listener-sponsored nonprofit community radio network with five radio stations and more than one hundred affiliate radio stations across the United States. KPFA 94.1 FM in Berkeley, California, the first Pacifica radio station, went on the air on April 15, 1949. The five stations—which also included KPFK 90.7 FM in Los Angeles, California; KPFT 90.1 FM in Houston, Texas; and WPFW FM in Washington, DC—reached out to communities marginalized in mainstream media. For more, see Phylis W. Johnson and Michael C. Keith, *Queer Airwaves: The Story of Gay and Lesbian Broadcasting*, 27.

52 Matthew Lasar, *Pacifica Radio*, xi.

53 Casillas, *Sounds of Belonging*, 63.

54 Ricardo Romano García, interview by author, April 11, 2014, Granger, Washington.

55 Karen Everhart, Mike Janssen, and Steve Behrens, "Timeline: The History of Public Broadcasting in the U.S.," *Current*, n.d., accessed May 5, 2021, https://current.org/timeline-the-history-of-public-broadcasting-in-the-u-s/.

56 Casillas first introduced the importance of these task forces to the development of Chicano public radio. For an extensive discussion of the task forces, see Casillas, *Sounds of Belonging*, 63–64.

57 Task Force on Minorities in Public Broadcasting, *A Formula for Change: The Report of the Task Force on Minorities in Public Broadcasting*.

58 For more on this study, see Caroline Isber and Muriel Cantor, *Report of the Task Force on Women in Public Broadcasting*, 1975.

59 Corporation for Public Broadcasting, *Special Circumstances, Special Needs Report*, 10.

60 Isber and Cantor, *Report of the Task Force on Women in Public Broadcasting*. Radio scholar Casillas first cited the importance of the Women in Public Broadcasting Task Force and the Task Force on Minorities in Public Broadcasting reports, which were led by Dr. Gloria Anderson, in *Sounds of Belonging*, 63.

61 Chávez, "Emerging Media."

62 Northwest Chicano Radio Network Articles of Incorporation, April 27, 1976. Courtesy of Rosa Ramón.

63 Prior to receiving the designated call letters of KDNA, the radio station is often referred to as "Cadena" in archival documents.

64 A subsidiary communications authorization (SCA) is a subcarrier on a radio station allowing the station to broadcast additional services as part of its signal. KRAB FM was the fourth noncommercial station in the United States. For a rich online archive of KRAB's history, see "KRAB-FM 107.7 Seattle, Washington 1962–1984," last modified March 18, 2021, accessed May 4, 2021, http://krab.fm/.

65 Rillmond Schear, "Rabble's Babble, Hot Licks by Bix," *Seattle Magazine*, June 1, 1964, KRAB archive, http://www.krabarchive.com/krab-primary-sources-and -links.html#seattlemag1964.

66 Schear, "Rabble's Babble."

67 "Edición Especial" ("Special Edition"), *Radio KDNA Program Guide*, November 16 to December 16, 1979, courtesy of Rosa Ramón.

68 Susan Marionneaux, "KDNA Radio's Estella Del Villar Breaks Gender Barriers with a Strong Voice," *Yakima Herald-Republic*, June 22, 2000.

69 Chávez, "Emerging Media."

70 Rosa Ramón, interview by author, March 9, 2012, Seattle, Washington.

71 Rosa Ramón, interview by author, March 9, 2012, Seattle, Washington.

72 María Martin, telephone interview by author, February 24, 2014, Seattle, Washington.

73 Ricardo Romano García, interview by author, April 11, 2014, Granger, Washington.

74 Ricardo Romano García, interview by author, April 11, 2014, Granger, Washington.

75 "Ondas en Español de Primavera" ("Springtime Spanish Airwaves"), *Radio KDNA Program Guide*, 1980, courtesy of Rosa Ramón.

76 "Ondas en Español de Primavera" ("Springtime Spanish Airwaves"), *Radio KDNA Program Guide*, 1980, courtesy of Rosa Ramón.

77 Ricardo Romano García, interview by author, April 11, 2014, Granger, Washington.

78 Casillas, *Sounds of Belonging*, 5.

79 *Yakima Herald-Republic*, December 17, 1984.

80 Rosa Ramón, interview by author, March 9, 2012, Seattle, Washington.

81 Amelia Ramón, interview by author, April 12, 2014, Granger, Washington.

82 Ricardo Romano García, interview by author, April 11, 2014, Granger, Washington.

83 Rosa Ramón, interview by author, March 9, 2012, Seattle, Washington.

84 Ricardo Romano García, interview by author, April 11, 2014, Granger, Washington.

85 "Ondas en Español de Primavera" ("Springtime Spanish Airwaves"), *Radio KDNA Program Guide,* 1980, courtesy of Rosa Ramón.

86   Gaye Theresa Johnson, *Spaces of Conflict, Sounds of Solidarity: Music, Race, and Spatial Entitlement in Los Angeles*, x.

87   Johnson, *Spaces of Conflict, Sounds of Solidarity*, x.

88   Gamboa, *Mexican Labor and World War II*, xix.

CHAPTER 2: BROTANDO DEL SILENCIO

Epigraphs: *Women of Radio KDNA*, a ten-minute audio recording digitized and shared with me by Rosa Ramón, was produced for a women's conference in 1984 that details the work of women at the radio station. The segment highlights three radio producers—María Estela Rebollosa, Celia Prieto, and Estella Del Villar—with host Rosa Ramón, who takes listeners on a sonic walk-through of the Radio Cadena station studios in Granger, Washington. Courtesy of Rosa Ramón.

1   Dolores Inés Casillas, *Sounds of Belonging: U.S. Spanish-Language Radio and Public Advocacy*.

2   *Reflexión (Reflection)* public broadcasting television program recorded and produced in December 1980 by ABC channel 35 in Yakima. Digital recording courtesy of Rosa Ramón.

3   *Women of Radio KDNA* program, 1984, courtesy of Rosa Ramón.

4   Thank you to the collective listening group of the *Women of Radio KDNA* segment: Ivette Bayo, alma khasawnih, Noralis Rodríguez-Coss, and Miriam Valdovinos-Smith.

5   Maylei Blackwell, *¡Chicana Power! Contested Histories of Feminism in the Chicano Movement*, 165.

6   Chicana feminist scholar Maylei Blackwell's own sonic treasure came from a recording of a radio program hosted by Chicana activist Irma Barrera. Blackwell reflects on the impact of listening to this recording: "As the recording played," Blackwell describes with awe, "we heard the Chicano clap and the momentum building with a long litany of 'Vivas!' " *¡Chicana Power!*, 165. Just as this recording provided a new sonic understanding of the 1971 Conferencia de Mujeres por la Raza (Conference for Women of the People) in Houston, the *Women of Radio KDNA* program provides evidence of Chicana media practice and Chicana radio praxis. For more, see Blackwell, *¡Chicana Power!*, 165.

7   Rosa Ramón, interview by author, March 9, 2012, Seattle, Washington.

8   Rosa Ramón, interview by author, March 9, 2012, Seattle, Washington.

9   See Blackwell, *¡Chicana Power!*; Dionne Espinoza, " 'Revolutionary Sisters': Women's Solidarity and Collective Identification among Chicana Brown"; Dolores Delgado Bernal, "Disrupting Epistemological Boundaries: Reflections on Feminista Methodological and Pedagogical Interventions"; and Dionne Espinoza, María Eugenia Cotera, and Maylei Blackwell, eds., *Chicana Movidas: New Narratives of Activism and Feminism in the Movement Era*.

10   Alma García, *Chicana Feminist Thought: The Basic Historical Writings*, 5.

11 Angie Chabram, "I Throw Punches for My Race, but I Don't Want to Be a Man: Writing Us—Chica-nos (Girl, Us)/Chicanas—into the Movement Script," 88.

12 Chela Sandoval, *Methodology of the Oppressed.*

13 Jillian M. Báez, *In Search of Belonging: Latinas, Media, and Citizenship.*

14 Báez, *In Search of Belonging,* 16.

15 Guerrero and Ramón, "Mujeres in Public Radio."

16 Guerrero and Ramón, "Mujeres in Public Radio."

17 Dionne Espinoza, " 'The Partido Belongs to Those Who Will Work for It': Chicana Organizing and Leadership in the Texas Raza Unida Party, 1970–1980," 196.

18 Espinoza, " 'The Partido Belongs to Those Who Will Work for It'."

19 Bernice Zuniga, interview by author, May 2019, Tempe, Arizona.

20 Caroline Isber and Muriel G. Cantor, *Report of the Task Force on Women in Public Broadcasting.*

21 *Women of Radio KDNA* program, 1984, courtesy of Rosa Ramón.

22 *Women of Radio KDNA* program, 1984, courtesy of Rosa Ramón.

23 Kate Lacey and Michele Hilmes, "Editors' Introduction," 2.

24 Muriel G. Cantor, "Women and Public Broadcasting," 17.

25 *Women of Radio KDNA* program, 1984, courtesy of Rosa Ramón.

26 *Women of Radio KDNA* program, 1984, courtesy of Rosa Ramón.

27 *Women of Radio KDNA* program, 1984, courtesy of Rosa Ramón.

28 *Women of Radio KDNA* program, 1984, courtesy of Rosa Ramón.

29 *Women of Radio KDNA* program, 1984, courtesy of Rosa Ramón.

30 Susan J. Douglas, *Listening In: Radio and the American Imagination,* 233.

31 Rosa Ramón, interview by author, March 9, 2012, Seattle, Washington.

32 Mary Wairimu Gatua, Tracey Owens Patton, and Michael R. Brown, "Giving Voice to Invisible Women: 'FIRE' as Model of a Successful Women's Community Radio in Africa," 166.

33 María Martin, telephone interview by author, February 24, 2014.

34 Michelle Habell-Pallán, "Chicana Soundscapes: Introduction," *Sounding Out!* blog, August 28, 2017, https://soundstudiesblog.com/2017/08/28/introduction-to-chicana-soundscapes-forum/.

35 Angela Y. Davis, "Introduction: An Archive of Feminist Activism," 7.

36 Sonia Saldívar-Hull, *Feminisms on the Border: Chicana Gender Politics and Literature,* 161.

37 Esperanze Graff, *Buenas Noches,* "Mujer," October 5, 1982, KDNA, American Archive of Public Broadcasting, GBH and Library of Congress, Boston, MA, and Washington, DC, accessed April 9, 2021, http://americanarchive.org/catalog/cpb-aacip-199-22h7ovfq.

38 *Women of Radio KDNA* program, 1984, courtesy of Rosa Ramón.

39 Susan Marionneaux, "KDNA Radio's Estella Del Villar Breaks Gender Barriers with a Strong Voice," *Yakima Herald-Republic,* June 22, 2000.

40 *Women of Radio KDNA* program, 1984, courtesy of Rosa Ramón.

41 Rosa Ramón, interview by author, March 9, 2012, Seattle, Washington.

42 Rosa Ramón, interview by author, March 9, 2012, Seattle, Washington.

43 *Women of Radio KDNA* program, 1984, courtesy of Rosa Ramón.

CHAPTER 3. RADIO RASQUACHE

1   Soul Rebel Radio, *The Life, Legacy, and Contradictions of Che Guevara*, originally aired on KPFK 90.7 FM, May 2008.

2   Women Who Rock Collective cemented my own DIY or "do it with others" cultural practice to creating media. For more on my experiences with this collective, see Michelle Habell-Pallán, Sonnet Retman, Angelica Macklin, and Monica De La Torre, "Women Who Rock: Making Scenes, Building Communities: Convivencia and Archivista Praxis for a Digital Era."

3   Tomás Ybarra-Frausto, *Rasquachismo: A Chicano Sensibility*; Amalia Mesa Baines, "Domesticana: The Sensibility of Chicana Rasquachismo."

4   Stacy I. Macías, "Claiming Style, Consuming Culture: The Politics of Latina Self-Styling and Fashion Lines"; Marviel T. Danielson, "Bodies in Motion: Latina/o Popular culture as Rasquache Resistance."

5   Rosa Linda Fregoso, *MeXicana Encounters: The Making of Social Identities on the Borderlands*.

6   Laura Pérez, *Chicana Art: The Politics of Spiritual and Aesthetic Altarities*, 7.

7   Michelle Habell-Pallán, *Loca Motion: The Travels of Chicana and Latina Popular Culture*, 200.

8   Habell-Pallán, *Loca Motion*, 200.

9   Habell-Pallán, *Loca Motion*, 49.

10 Neil Verma, *Theater of the Mind: Imagination, Aesthetics, and American Radio Drama*, 35.

11 Christina Dunbar-Hester, *Low Power to the People: Pirates, Protests, and Politics in FM Radio Activism*, x.

12 *Tres Hombres Sin Fronteras*, episode one: "Una Nueva Vida" ("A New Life"). This is a radio program recorded in 1989 in California, produced by Novela Health Foundation and KDNA.

13 Families with mixed immigration statuses and even US citizens were shuttled back to Mexico during these historical moments of anti-immigrant and anti-Mexican legislation like Mexican and Mexican American repatriation in the 1930s and Operation Wetback in 1954. For more on these programs and its effects on Mexican communities, see George J. Sánchez, *Becoming Mexican American: Ethnicity, Culture, and Identity in Chicano Los Angeles, 1900–1945*.

14 A 1990 study by Merrill Singer et al., "SIDA: The Economic, Social, and Cultural Context of AIDS among Latinos," found that most AIDS/HIV prevention materials for Latinos were lacking in cultural sensitivity and were not the appropriate reading level in Spanish. Materials that did exist were often poorly disseminated.

15 Singer et al., "SIDA," 86.

16 Singer et al., "SIDA."

17 Bernadette Lalonde, Peter Rabinowitz, Mary Lou Shefsky, and Kathleen Washienko, "La Esperanza Del Valle: Alcohol Prevention Novelas for Hispanic Youth and Their Families."

18 Carolina Acosta-Alzuru, " 'I'm Not a Feminist . . . I Only Defend Women as Human Beings': The Production, Representation, and Consumption of Feminism in a Telenovela."

19 Jonathan Sterne, *The Sound Studies Reader*, 6.

20 Ricardo Romano García, interview by author, April 11, 2014, Granger, Washington.

21 Ricardo Romano García, interview by author, April 11, 2014, Granger, Washington.

22 Scott Maier, "Soap Operas Help in Fight against AIDS," *Seattle Post-Intelligencer*, January 7, 1991.

23 Claudia Puig, "Radio Playlet Dramatizes AIDS Danger to Latinos," *Los Angeles Times*, February 26, 1990.

24 Maier, "Soap Operas Help in Fight against AIDS."

25 Dolores Inés Casillas, *Sounds of Belonging: U.S. Spanish-Language Radio and Public Advocacy*, 5.

26 Kimberlé Crenshaw, "Mapping the Margins: Intersectionality, Identity Politics, and Violence against Women of Color."

27 Shiraz I. Mishra, Ross F. Conner, and J. Raul Magana, eds., *AIDS Crossing Borders: The Spread of HIV among Migrant Latinos*, 50.

28 Singer et al., "SIDA," 86.

29 Singer et al., "SIDA."

30 Singer et al., "SIDA."

31 *Tres Hombres Sin Fronteras.*

32 Cherrie Moraga, "La Güera," in *Loving in the War Years: Lo Que Nunca Paso por Sus Labios.*

33 Moraga, "A Long Line of Vendidas," in *Loving in the War Years*, 82.

34 Michelle Habell-Pallán, "Chicana Soundscapes: Introduction," *Sounding Out!* blog, August 28, 2017, https://soundstudiesblog.com/2017/08/28/introduction-to-chicana-soundscapes-forum/.

35 Miguel Paredes Jr., "Spatial Practices of Soul Rebel Radio in Los Angeles' Third World Left."

36 Paredes Jr., "Spatial Practices of Soul Rebel Radio."

37 Paredes Jr., "Spatial Practices of Soul Rebel Radio."

38 Martha Gonzalez, "Caminos y Canciones en Los Angeles, California."

39 Dunbar-Hester, *Low Power to the People.*

40 Latina bodies have historically been a testing site for contraceptives (Puerto Rico) and have even been forcefully sterilized against their knowledge. See Elena R. Gutiérrez, *Fertile Matters: The Politics of Mexican-Origin Women's Reproduction.*

41 Laura Cambron and Monica De La Torre, *The Young Women's Show*, "Gardasil Skit" script excerpt, Soul Rebel Radio, October 2008.

42 David Reyes and Tom Waldman, *Land of a Thousand Dances: Chicano Rock 'n' Roll from Southern California.*

43 Media Bureau Chief, *Report on Ownership of Commercial Broadcast Stations*, Federal Communications Commission, June 27, 2014.

44 Media Bureau Chief, *Report on Ownership of Commercial Broadcast Stations.*
45 Diosa Femme and Mala Muñoz, *Locatora Radio*, accessed May 5, 2021, https://locatoraradio.com/. Esther Díaz Martín theorizes the work of *Locatora Radio* as "radiophonic feminisms," which underscores the sonic construction of feminist epistemologies; for more, see "Radiophonic Feminisms: The Sounds and Voices of Contemporary Latina Radio Hosts in the U.S. Southwest, 1990–2017."
46 Macías, "Claiming Style, Consuming Culture," 407.
47 Gloria Anzaldúa, *Borderlands/La Frontera: The New Mestiza.*
48 Catherine S. Ramírez, *The Woman in the Zoot Suit: Gender, Nationalism, and the Cultural Politics of Memory.*
49 Femme and Muñoz, "Loquitas Anonymous" video, Locatora Radio, November 2, 2019, accessed May 5, 2021, https://locatoraradio.com/loquitas-anonymous.
50 *Locatora Radio* tweets at the *Los Angeles Times*, May 20, 2020, https://twitter.com/Locatora_Radio/status/1263329649565724672.
51 *Locatora Radio* tweet, May 20, 2020, Twitter @Locatora_Radio, https://twitter.com/Locatora_Radio/status/1263329649565724672.
52 Stephanie Mendez, "A Latina Void in Podcasting? The Women of 'Locatora Radio' Are All Over That." *Los Angeles Times*, September 23, 2020.

EPILOGUE

1 Cantinflas is the stage name for Mexican comedian, actor, producer, and screenwriter Mario Moreno. A beloved icon in Mexican and Chicano popular culture, Cantinflas's humor centers working-class subjectivities.
2 Ricardo Romano García, interview by author, April 11, 2014, Granger, Washington.
3 Dolores Delgado Bernal, "Disrupting Epistemological Boundaries: Reflections on Feminista Methodological and Pedagogical Interventions."
4 Patricia Zavella, "Feminist Insider Dilemmas: Constructing Ethnic Identity with 'Chicana' Informants," 54.
5 Monica De La Torre, "Sonic Bridging, Locating, Archiving, and Preserving Spanish-Language and Bilingual Radio in the United States."
6 María Cotera, "Nuestra Autohistoria: Toward a Chicana Digital Praxis."
7 John Vallier, "Sound Archiving Close to Home: Why Community Partnerships Matter," 39.
8 Monica De La Torre, Julio César Guerrero, and Rosa Ramón, "Radio KDNA 41st Anniversary Panel"; Monica De La Torre and Rosa Ramón, "Spanish Language and Multilingual Radio."

BIBLIOGRAPHY

PRIMARY SOURCES

Cambron, Laura, and Monica De La Torre. *The Young Women's Show*. Single radio program recorded October 2008, Los Angeles, produced by Soul Rebel Radio. KPFK 90.7 FM digital recording. Courtesy of Monica De La Torre.

Corporation for Public Broadcasting. *Special Circumstances, Special Needs Report*. Corporation for Public Broadcasting records, Special Collections and University Archives, University of Maryland Libraries, College Park, n.d.

De La Torre, Monica, Julio César Guerrero, and Rosa Ramón. "Radio KDNA 41st Anniversary Panel." Hosted virtually by MeXicanos 2070, December 17, 2020.

De La Torre, Monica, and Rosa Ramón. "Spanish Language and Multilingual Radio." Panel presentation at the Radio Preservation Task Force Conference: From Archive to Classroomat the Library of Congress, Washington, DC, November 2–4, 2017.

García, Ricardo Romano. Interview by author, April 11, 2014, Granger, Washington. Author's collection.

Isber, Caroline, and Muriel G. Cantor. *Report of the Task Force on Women in Public Broadcasting*. Washington, DC: Corporation for Public Broadcasting, 1975.

Los Chicanos de Seattle (The Chicanos of Seattle). Film directed by Jack Forman, KOMO-ABC News, Seattle, 1973.

Martin, María. Telephone interview by author, February 24, 2014. Author's collection.

O'Neill, Anne, and Sharon Walker. "Tomás Villanueva, Founder, United Farm Workers of Washington State." Interviews on April 11, 2003, and June 7, 2004. Accessed December 15, 2020. Seattle Civil Rights and Labor History Project, University of Washington. http://depts.washington.edu/civilr/villanueva.htm.

Ramón, Amelia. Interview by author, April 12, 2014, Granger, Washington. Author's collection.

Ramón, Rosa. Interview by author, March 9, 2012, Seattle, Washington. Author's collection.

Reflexión (Reflection). Public broadcasting television program recorded 1980. Digital recording. Courtesy of Rosa Ramón.

Reinsch, Charles (Chuck). Interview by author, July 18, 2017, Seattle, Washington. Author's collection.

Task Force on Minorities in Public Broadcasting. *A Formula for Change: The Report of the Task Force on Minorities in Public Broadcasting.* Washington, DC: Corporation for Public Broadcasting, 1978.

Tres Hombres Sin Fronteras. Radio program recorded in 1989 in California, produced by Novela Health Foundation and Radio KDNA. Audiocassette. Courtesy of Rosa Ramón.

Women of Radio KDNA. Single program recorded in 1984, Granger, Washington. Digital recording. Courtesy of Rosa Ramón.

Zuniga, Bernice. Interview by author, May 2019, Tempe, Arizona. Author's collection.

SECONDARY SOURCES

Acosta-Alzuru, Carolina. " ' I'm Not a Feminist . . . I Only Defend Women as Human Beings': The Production, Representation, and Consumption of Feminism in a Telenovela." *Critical Studies in Media Communication* 20, no. 3 (September 1, 2003): 269–94. https://doi.org/10.1080/07393180302775.

Aguilar, Ernesto. "Ernesto Aguilar: I'm a Testament to Public Media's Transformative Power." *Current*, April 2017, accessed May 20, 2019. https://current.org/2017/04/ernesto-aguilar-im-a-testament-to-public-medias-transformative-power/.

Aguirre, Michael D. "Excavating the Chicano Movement: Chicana Feminism, Mobilization, and Leadership at El Centro de la Raza, 1972–1979." In *Chicana Movidas: New Narratives of Activism and Feminism in the Movement Era*, edited by Dionne Espinoza, María Eugenia Cotera, and Maylei Blackwell, 174–88. Austin: University of Texas Press, 2018.

Alaniz, Yolanda, and Megan Cornish. *Viva La Raza: A History of Chicano Identity and Resistance.* Seattle: Red Letter Press, 2008.

Anzaldúa, Gloria. *Borderlands/La Frontera: The New Mestiza.* San Francisco: Spinsters/Aunt Lute, 1987.

Avery, Robert K. "The Public Broadcasting Act of 1967: Looking Ahead by Looking Back." *Critical Studies in Media Communication* 24, no. 4 (2007): 358–64.

Báez, Jillian M. *In Search of Belonging: Latinas, Media, and Citizenship.* Urbana: University of Illinois Press, 2018.

Baines, Amalia Mesa. "Domesticana: The Sensibility of Chicana Rasquachismo." In *Chicana Feminisms: A Critical Reader*, edited by Patricia Zavella, Gabriela F. Arredondo, Aida Hurtado, Norma Klahn, and Olga Nájera-Ramírez, 298–317. Durham, NC: Duke University Press, 2003.

Barlow, William. "Rebel Airways: Radio and Revolution in Latin America." *Howard Journal of Communications* 2, no. 2 (1990): 123.

Bernal, Dolores Delgado. "Disrupting Epistemological Boundaries: Reflections on Feminista Methodological and Pedagogical Interventions." *Aztlán: Journal of Chicano Studies* 45, no. 1 (2020): 155–70.

———. "Grassroots Leadership Reconceptualized: Chicana Oral Histories and the 1968 East Los Angeles School Blowouts." *Frontiers: Journal of Women Studies* 19, no. 2 (1998): 113–42.

Berríos-Miranda, Marisol, Shannon Dudley, and Michelle Habell-Pallán. *American Sabor: Latinos and Latinas in US Popular Music / Latinos y Latinas En La Musica Popular Estadounidense*. Seattle: University of Washington Press, 2017.

Blackwell, Maylei. *¡Chicana Power! Contested Histories of Feminism in the Chicano Movement*. Austin: University of Texas Press, 2011.

Brady, Mary Pat. *Extinct Lands, Temporal Geographies: Chicana Literature and the Urgency of Space*. Durham, NC: Duke University Press, 2002.

Browne, Donald. "Speaking in Our Own Tongue: Linguistic Minority Radio in the United States." In *Radio Cultures: The Sound Medium in American Life*, edited by Michael C. Keith, 30. New York: Peter Lang Publishing, 2008.

Broyles-González, Yolanda. *El Teatro Campesino: Theater in the Chicano Movement*. Austin: University of Texas Press, 1994.

Cantor, Muriel G. "Women and Public Broadcasting." *Journal of Communication* 27, no. 1 (1977): 14–19.

Cantú, Norma E., and Olga Nájera-Ramírez. *Chicana Traditions: Continuity and Change*. Urbana: University of Illinois Press, 2002.

Casillas, Dolores Inés. *Sounds of Belonging: U.S. Spanish-Language Radio and Public Advocacy*. New York: New York University Press, 2014.

———. "Sounds of Surveillance: U.S. Spanish-Language Radio Patrols La Migra." *American Quarterly* 63, no. 3 (2011): 807–29.

———. "US Spanish-Language Radio." Oxford Bibliographies, Latino Studies, 2018.

Castañeda, Antonia I. " 'Que Se Pudieran Defender (So You Could Defend Yourselves)': Chicanas, Regional History, and National Discourses." *Frontiers: Journal of Women Studies* 22, no. 3 (2001): 116–42.

———. *Three Decades of Engendering History: Selected Works of Antonia I. Castaneda*. Denton: University of North Texas Press, 2014.

Castañeda, Oscar Rosales. "Timeline: Movimiento from 1960–1985." Seattle Civil Rights and Labor History Project, n.d., Civil Rights and Labor History Consortium, University of Washington, accessed May 5, 2021. http://depts.washington .edu/civilr/mecha_timeline.htm.

Castañeda Paredes, Mari. "Altering the U.S. Soundscape through Latina/o Community Radio." In *The Routledge Companion to Latina/o Media*, edited by Maria Elena Cepeda and Dolores Inés Casillas, 110–22. London: Routledge, Taylor & Francis Group, 2016.

———. "The Transformation of Spanish-Language Radio in the U.S." *Journal of Radio Studies* 10, no. 1 (2003): 5–16.

Chabram, Angie. "I Throw Punches for My Race, but I Don't Want to Be a Man: Writing Us—Chica-nos (Girl, Us)/Chicanas—into the Movement Script." In *Cultural Studies*, edited by Lawrence Grossberg, Cary Nelson, and Paula A. Treichler, 81–95. New York: Routledge, 1992.

Chávez, Ramón. "Emerging Media: A History and Analysis of Chicano Communication Efforts in Washington State." Master's thesis, University of Washington, Seattle, 1979.

Cotera, María. "Nuestra Autohistoria: Toward a Chicana Digital Praxis." *American Quarterly* 70, no. 3 (2018): 483–504.

Crenshaw, Kimberlé. "Mapping the Margins: Intersectionality, Identity Politics, and Violence against Women of Color." *Stanford Law Review* 43, no. 6 (1991): 1241–99.

Cruz, Sonia De La. "Latino Airwaves: Radio Bilingüe and Spanish-Language Public Radio." *Journal of Radio and Audio Media* 24, no. 2 (July 3, 2017): 226–37.

Danielson, Marviel T. "Bodies in Motion: Latina/o Popular Culture as Rasquache Resistance." In *The Routledge Companion to Latina/o Popular Culture*, edited by Frederick Luis Aldama, 392–406. London: Routledge, 2016.

Davis, Angela Y. "Introduction: An Archive of Feminist Activism." In *Feminist Freedom Warriors: Genealogies, Justice, Politics, and Hope*, edited by Chandra Talpade Mohanty and Linda E. Carty, 7–15. Chicago: Haymarket Books, 2018.

De La Torre, Monica. "Feminista Frequencies: Chicana Radio Activism in the Pacific Northwest, 1975–1990." In *Chicana Movidas: New Narratives of Activism and Feminism in the Movement Era*, edited by Dionne Espinoza, María Eugenia Cotera, and Maylei Blackwell, 159–73. Austin: University of Texas Press, 2018.

———. " 'Programas Sin Vergüenza (Shameless Programs)': Mapping Chicanas in Community Radio in the 1970s." *Women's Studies Quarterly* 43, no. 3–4 (2015): 175–90.

———. "Sonic Bridging: Locating, Archiving, and Preserving Spanish-Language and Bilingual Radio in the United States." *New Review of Film and Television Studies* 16, no. 4 (2018): 446–53.

Delgadillo, Theresa. *Latina Lives in Milwaukee.* Champaign: University of Illinois Press, 2015.

Díaz Martín, Esther. "Radiophonic Feminisms: The Sounds and Voices of Contemporary Latina Radio Hosts in the U.S. Southwest, 1990–2017." Diss., University of Texas, Austin, 2018. https://doi.org/10.15781/T23F4M642.

Douglas, Susan J. *Listening In: Radio and the American Imagination.* Minneapolis: University of Minnesota Press, 2004.

Dunbar-Hester, Christina. *Low Power to the People: Pirates, Protest, and Politics in FM Radio Activism.* Cambridge, MA: MIT Press, 2014.

Engelman, Ralph. *Public Radio and Television in America: A Political History.* Thousand Oaks, CA: Sage Publications, 1996.

Espinoza, Dionne. " 'The Partido Belongs to Those Who Will Work for It': Chicana Organizing and Leadership in the Texas Raza Unida Party, 1970–1980." *Aztlán: Journal of Chicano Studies* 36, no. 1 (2011): 191–210.

———. " 'Revolutionary Sisters': Women's Solidarity and Collective Identification among Chicana Brown." *Aztlán: Journal of Chicano Studies* 26, no. 1 (2001): 17–58.

Espinoza, Dionne, María Eugenia Cotera, and Maylei Blackwell, eds. *Chicana Movidas: New Narratives of Activism and Feminism in the Movement Era.* Austin: University of Texas Press, 2018.

Estrada, Josué Quezada. "Texas Mexican Diaspora to Washington State: Recruitment, Migration, and Community, 1940–1960." Master's thesis, Washington State University, Pullman, 2007.

Fowler, Gene, and Bill Crawford. *Border Radio: Quacks, Yodelers, Pitchmen, Psychics, and Other Amazing Broadcasters of the American Airwaves.* Austin: University of Texas Press, 2002.

Fregoso, Rosa Linda. *The Bronze Screen: Chicana and Chicano Film Culture.* Minneapolis: University of Minnesota Press, 1993.

———. *MeXicana Encounters: The Making of Social Identities on the Borderlands.* Berkeley: University of California Press, 2003.

Gamboa, Erasmo. "Chicanos in the Pacific Northwest: Expanding the Discourse." *Americas Review* 23, no. 3–4 (1995): 15–25.

———. *Mexican Labor and World War II: Braceros in the Pacific Northwest, 1942–1947.* Seattle: University of Washington Press, 2000.

———. "Mexican Migration into Washington State: A History, 1940–1950." *Pacific Northwest Quarterly* 72, no. 3 (1981): 121–31.

———. *Voces Hispanas = Hispanic Voices of Idaho: Excerpts from the Idaho Hispanic Oral History Project.* Boise: Idaho Commission on Hispanic Affairs and Idaho Humanities Council, 1992.

García, Alma. *Chicana Feminist Thought: The Basic Historical Writings.* New York: Routledge, 1997.

García, Jerry, and Gilberto García, eds. *Memory, Community, and Activism: Mexican Migration and Labor in the Pacific Northwest.* East Lansing: Julian Samora Research Institute Books, distributed by Michigan State University Press, 2005.

García, Jerry, and Dora Sánchez Treviño. "A Chicana in Northern Aztlán: An Oral History of Dora Sánchez Treviño." *Frontiers: Journal of Women Studies* 19, no. 2 (1998): 16–52.

Gatua, Mary Wairimu, Tracey Owens Patton, and Michael R. Brown. "Giving Voice to Invisible Women: 'FIRE' as Model of a Successful Women's Community Radio in Africa." *Howard Journal of Communications* 21, no. 2 (2010): 164–81.

Gonzalez, Martha. "Caminos y Canciones en Los Ángeles, California." In *The Tide Was Always High: The Music of Latin America in Los Angeles*, edited by Josh Kun, 267–76. Oakland: University of California Press, 2017.

———. *Chican@ Artivistas: Music, Community, and Transborder Tactics in East Los Angeles.* Austin: University of Texas Press, 2020.

Guerrero, Julio César, and Rosa Ramón. "Mujeres in Public Radio." *La Voz: The News Magazine of the Concilio for the Spanish Speaking.* April 1984. University of Washington Libraries, Special Collections, Seattle.

Gutiérrez, Elena R. *Fertile Matters: The Politics of Mexican-Origin Women's Reproduction.* Austin: University of Texas Press, 2008.

Gutiérrez, Félix, and Jorge Reina Schement. *Spanish-Language Radio in the Southwestern United States.* Monograph no. 5, Center for Mexican American Studies, University of Texas, Austin, 1979.

Habell-Pallán, Michelle. *Loca Motion: The Travels of Chicana and Latina Popular Culture.* New York: New York University Press, 2005.

Habell-Pallán, Michelle, Sonnet Retman, Angelica Macklin, and Monica De La Torre. "Women Who Rock: Making Scenes, Building Communities: Convivencia and Archivista Praxis for a Digital Era." In *Routledge Companion to Media*

Studies and Digital Humanities, edited by Jentery Sayers, 67–77. New York: Routledge, 2018.

hooks, bell. *Talking Back: Thinking Feminist, Thinking Black*. Toronto, ON: Between the Lines, 1989.

Jimenez, Carlos. "Antenna Dilemmas: The Rise of an Indigenous-Language Low-Power Radio Station in Southern California." *Journal of Radio and Audio Media* 26, no. 2 (July 3, 2019): 247–69.

Johnson, Gaye Theresa. *Spaces of Conflict, Sounds of Solidarity: Music, Race, and Spatial Entitlement in Los Angeles*. Berkeley: University of California Press, 2013.

Johnson, Phylis W., and Michael C. Keith. *Queer Airwaves: The Story of Gay and Lesbian Broadcasting*. Armonk, NY: M. E. Sharpe, 2011.

Keeler, Amanda, and Josh Shepperd. "Radio Research as Critical Archival Studies: Cross-Sector Collaboration and the Sound Record." *Journal of Radio and Audio Media* 26 (2019): 1, 4–7.

Lacey, Kate. *Feminine Frequencies: Gender, German Radio, and the Public Sphere, 1923–1945*. Ann Arbor: University of Michigan Press, 1996.

Lacey, Kate, and Michele Hilmes. "Editors' Introduction." *Feminist Media Histories* 1, no. 4 (2015): 2.

Lalonde, Bernadette, Peter Rabinowitz, Mary Lou Shefsky, and Kathleen Washienko. "La Esperanza Del Valle: Alcohol Prevention Novelas for Hispanic Youth and Their Families." *Health Education and Behavior* 24, no. 5 (1997): 587–602.

Lasar, Matthew. *Pacifica Radio*. 2nd ed. Philadelphia, PA: Temple University Press, 2000.

Latina Feminist Group. *Telling to Live: Latina Feminist Testimonios*. Durham, NC: Duke University Press, 2001.

Lewels, Francisco J. *The Uses of the Media by the Chicano Movement: A Study in Minority Access*. Westport, CT: Praeger Publishers, 1974.

Lochte, Bob. "U.S. Public Radio: What Is It—and for Whom?" In *More Than a Music Box: Radio Cultures and Communities in a Multi-Media World*, edited by Andrew Crisell, 40. New York: Berghahn Books, 2006.

Loreck, Janice. "Pleasurable Critiques: Feminist Viewership and Criticism in Feminist Frequency, Jezebel, and Rosie Recaps." *Feminist Media Studies* 18, no. 2 (March 4, 2018): 264–77.

Macías, Stacy I. "Claiming Style, Consuming Culture: The Politics of Latina Self-Styling and Fashion Lines." In *The Routledge Companion to Latina/o Popular Culture*, edited by Frederick Luis Aldama, 407–20. London: Routledge, 2016.

Maldonado, Carlos S., and Gilberto García. *The Chicano Experience in the Northwest*. Dubuque, IA: Kendall/Hunt Publishing Co., 1995.

Marez, Curtis. *Farm Worker Futurism: Speculative Technologies of Resistance*. Reprint ed. Minneapolis: University of Minnesota Press, 2016.

Martin, María. "Crossing Borders." In *Reality Radio: Telling True Stories in Sound*, edited by John Biewen and Alexa Dilworth, 157–64. Chapel Hill: University of North Carolina Press, 2010.

Mishra, Shiraz I., Ross F. Conner, and J. Raul Magana, eds. *AIDS Crossing Borders: The Spread of HIV among Migrant Latinos*. Boulder, CO: Westview Press, 1996.

Moraga, Cherrie. *Loving in the War Years: Lo Que Nunca Paso por Sus Labios*. 2nd ed. Boston, MA: South End Press, 2000.

Noriega, Chon A. *Shot in America: Television, the State, and the Rise of Chicano Cinema*. Minneapolis: University of Minnesota Press, 2000.

Ontiveros, Randy J. *In the Spirit of a New People: The Cultural Politics of the Chicano Movement*. New York: New York University Press, 2013.

Pardo, Mary. *Mexican American Women Activists*. Illustrated ed. Philadelphia, PA: Temple University Press, 1998.

Paredes, Miguel, Jr. "Spatial Practices of Soul Rebel Radio in Los Angeles' Third World Left." Master's thesis, California State University, Northridge, 2012. http://scholarworks.calstate.edu/handle/10211.2/1923.

Pérez, Emma. *The Decolonial Imaginary: Writing Chicanas into History*. Bloomington: Indiana University Press, 1999.

Pérez, Laura. *Chicana Art: The Politics of Spiritual and Aesthetic Altarities*. Durham, NC: Duke University Press, 2007.

Ramírez, Catherine S. *The Woman in the Zoot Suit: Gender, Nationalism, and the Cultural Politics of Memory*. Durham, NC: Duke University Press, 2009.

Reyes, David, and Tom Waldman. *Land of a Thousand Dances: Chicano Rock 'n' Roll from Southern California*. Albuquerque: University of New Mexico Press, 1998.

Robles, Sonia. *Mexican Waves: Radio Broadcasting along Mexico's Northern Border, 1930–1950*. Tucson: University of Arizona Press, 2019.

Ruiz, Vicki L. *From Out of the Shadows: Mexican Women in Twentieth-Century America*. 10th ed. Oxford: Oxford University Press, 2008.

Saldívar-Hull, Sonia. *Feminisms on the Border: Chicana Gender Politics and Literature*. Berkeley: University of California Press, 2000.

Sánchez, George J. *Becoming Mexican American: Ethnicity, Culture, and Identity in Chicano Los Angeles, 1900–1945*. Oxford: Oxford University Press, 1995.

Sandoval, Chela. *Methodology of the Oppressed*. Minneapolis: University of Minnesota Press, 2000.

Sifuentez, Mario Jimenez. *Of Forests and Fields: Mexican Labor in the Pacific Northwest*. New Brunswick, NJ: Rutgers University Press, 2016.

Singer, Merrill, et al. "SIDA: The Economic, Social, and Cultural Context of AIDS among Latinos." *Medical Anthropology Quarterly* 4, no. 1 (1990): 72–114. https://doi.org/10.1525/maq.1990.4.1.02a00060.

Slatta, Richard W. "Chicanos in the Pacific Northwest: An Historical Overview of Oregon's Chicanos." *Aztlán: Journal of Chicano Studies* 6, no. 3 (1975): 327–40.

Slatta, Richard W., and Maxine P. Atkinson. "Chicanos in the Pacific Northwest: A Demographic and Socioeconomic Portrait." *Pacific Northwest Quarterly* 70, no. 4 (1979): 155–62.

Smiles, Deondre. "Listening to Native Radio." *International Journal of Listening* 33, no. 3 (2019): 142–47.

Squires, Catherine R. "Black Talk Radio: Defining Community Needs and Identity." *Harvard International Journal of Press/Politics* 5, no. 2 (March 1, 2000): 73–95.

Sterne, Jonathan. *The Sound Studies Reader.* New York: Routledge, 2012.

Vallier, John. "Sound Archiving Close to Home: Why Community Partnerships Matter." *Notes: Quarterly Journal of Music Library Association* 67, no. 1 (2010): 39–49.

Vargas, Deborah R. *Dissonant Divas in Chicana Music: The Limits of La Onda.* Minneapolis: University of Minnesota Press, 2012.

Verma, Neil. *Theater of the Mind: Imagination, Aesthetics, and American Radio Drama.* Chicago: University of Chicago Press, 2012.

Ybarra-Frausto, Tomás. *Rasquachismo: A Chicano Sensibility.* Phoenix, AZ: Movimiento Artístico del Rio Salado (MARS), 1989.

Zavella, Patricia. "Feminist Insider Dilemmas: Constructing Ethnic Identity with 'Chicana' Informants." *Frontiers: Journal of Women Studies* 13, no. 3 (1993): 53–76.

INDEX

DECOLONIZING FEMINISMS
Piya Chatterjee, Series Editor

Humanizing the Sacred: Sisters in Islam and the Struggle for Gender Justice in Malaysia, by Azza Basarudin

Power Interrupted: Antiracist and Feminist Activism inside the United Nations, by Sylvanna Falcón

Transnational Testimonios: The Politics of Collective Knowledge Production, by Patricia DeRocher

Asian American Feminisms and Women of Color Politics, edited by Lynn Fujiwara and Shireen Roshanravan

Unruly Figures: Queerness, Sex Work, and the Politics of Sexuality in Kerala, by Navaneetha Mokkil

Resisting Disappearance: Military Occupation and Women's Activism in Kashmir, by Ather Zia

Tea and Solidarity: Tamil Women and Work in Postwar Sri Lanka, by Mythri Jegathesan

Axis of Hope: Iranian Women's Rights Activism across Borders, by Catherine Sameh

The Borders of AIDS: Race, Quarantine, and Resistance, by Karma R. Chávez

Making Livable Worlds: Afro–Puerto Rican Women Building Environmental Justice, by Hilda Lloréns

Feminista Frequencies: Community Building through Radio in the Yakima Valley, by Monica De La Torre

Dancing Transnational Feminisms: Ananya Dance Theatre and the Art of Social Justice, edited by Ananya Chatterjea, Hui Wilcox, and Alessandra Williams